WAYNE ROBINS

1968

INTRODUCTION

THE SUMMER OF LOVE
GIVES WAY TO
THE YEAR OF LIVING
DANGEROUSLY

n New Year's Day 1968, daredevil Evel Knievel tried to jump a motorcycle 151 feet over the fountains of Caesar's Palace. His crash landing put him in a coma for thirty days. He broke more bones than anyone knew the human body had.

It turned out to be a sign of things to come, because the next 364 days were like that for almost everyone else.

It was a year of living dangerously, and dying tragically. Assassins' bullets felled Martin Luther King Jr. and Robert F. Kennedy. President Lyndon B. Johnson stunned the country by deciding not to run for reelection. Vice President Hubert H. Humphrey was nominated at a convention in Chicago at which police beat protesters in the city's parks and journalists inside the convention hall.

As Country Joe McDonald sums it up: "America was a totalitarian state, and we were the enemy."

More than 10 percent of the ballots cast that November went to third-party candidate George Wallace, the racist governor of Alabama. The divided country elected Richard M. Nixon, who won on the promise that he would reestablish "law and order."

There was worldwide youth revolt. New York's Columbia University police dragged student demonstrators out of the buildings they had occupied. In Mexico City, authorities wantonly massacred student protesters. In France, the youth of Paris paralyzed the capitol and nearly overthrew Charles de Gaulle's government. The youth and student movement set loose when Czechoslovakia's Communist party tentatively eased its grip on the country was brutally crushed by a Soviet invasion. An unprecedented explosion of urban rage tore across America. Cities like Newark and Detroit never recovered.

Feminist protesters at the Miss America beauty pageant threw away their bras.

College students burned their draft cards.

It was that kind of year. An entire society seemed paranoid, manic-depressive, anxious.

The war in Vietnam was the dark thread that ran through it all.

"Looming in the back of every day's news is a sense that the country has gone berserk, that the country is committing an atrocious war, there doesn't seem to be any way to end it or even mitigate it," said author and NYU professor Todd Gitlin on National Public Radio's *Talk of the Nation*. "And in the background is the larger overhanging drama of the Cold War, the arms

race, the bomb, so that the whole history is shadowed by a sense of apocalypse that if not imminent is in any case a material possibility."

America and the rest of the world seemed on the eve of destruction. And popular music was the soundtrack as the year's wrenching newsreel played out. It absorbed the shrapnel diffusion of events, rewired pain into pleasure, and threw it back to a violently changing world in waves of pulsing rhythms, soulful shouts, and delirious screams of guitar feedback.

Somewhere between the June 1967 release of *Sgt. Pepper's Lonely Hearts Club Band* and the bloody Tet offensive in Vietnam, the Summer of Love ended and the emotional winter of 1968 began. Flower Power, to use the mass-media term, had begun to wilt. And those who had months earlier greeted friend and stranger alike with the two-fingered V sign for peace dropped the index finger, leaving the middle finger aloft to all comers. In 1967, the Beatles insisted that "All You Need is Love"; by 1968, however, the *White Album*'s "Helter Skelter" seemed a more appropriate accompaniment to a world on the brink of generational war.

You could, indeed, hear the change in the music. The soundtrack to the summer of 1967, the so-called Summer of Love, was buoyant, resilient, optimistic if naive. Heads rested on Jefferson Airplane's *Surrealistic Pillow*, a generation dreamed of "Somebody to Love," and hallucinated to "White Rabbit."

The Doors' "Light My Fire" was a scented candle in a darkened room. With the Rascals, it was easy to be "Groovin'"; with the Turtles, a breeze to be "Happy Together." By the end of 1967, however, songs like the Monkees' "Daydream Believer" seemed the province of teeny boppers alone.

As Dave Getz of the band Big Brother and the Holding Company says today, "I think 1968 might be the year when our generation might have had just the slight inkling beginning to happen that love, the love generation, and all of the, you know, the love that we were trying to bring came with pain...it's a package deal, you know?"

By 1968, wrote Greil Marcus in his book, *Mystery Train: Images of America in Rock and Roll,* "rock and roll was coming out of its San Francisco period...a fabulous euphoria in the

LOOMING IN THE BACK OF EVERY DAY'S NEWS IS A SENSE THAT THE COUNTRY HAS GONE BERSERK, THAT THE COUTRY IS COMMITTING AN ATROCIOUS WAR, THERE DOESN'T SEEM TO BE ANY WAY TO END IT OR EVEN MITIGATE IT.

middle of a war, innocence, and optimism running straight into the election of Richard Nixon." Rock had reached its first artistic—and, to quote Bob Dylan, "self-indulgent"—peak, and by 1968, as Marcus put it, "*Sgt. Pepper,* generally enshrined a year earlier as the greatest achievement in the history of popular music...now seemed very hollow..."

If *Sgt. Pepper* seemed at the time like an ephemeral epiphany it had also underlined the impact that rock and roll could have on the cul-

ture as a whole. Rock artists' appearances, their pronouncements and records had become psychic road maps, etiquette instructors, self-help and how-to books.

Bob Dylan was, of course, the prime exemplar of the rock and roll musician as oracle. And he threw many who had become accustomed to the baroque one-upmanship of the Beach Boys, Beatles, and Rolling Stones by releasing, between Christmas and New Year's 1968, *John Wesley Harding.* The album's strange wisdom

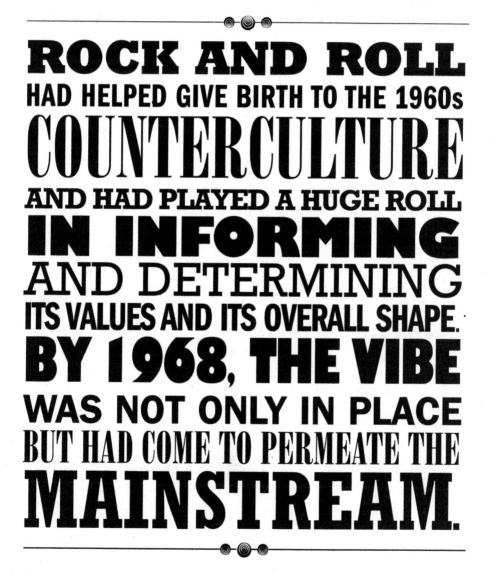

ROCK AND ROLL
HAD HELPED GIVE BIRTH TO THE 1960s
COUNTERCULTURE
AND HAD PLAYED A HUGE ROLL
IN INFORMING
AND DETERMINING
ITS VALUES AND ITS OVERALL SHAPE.
BY 1968, THE VIBE
WAS NOT ONLY IN PLACE
BUT HAD COME TO PERMEATE THE
MAINSTREAM.

tales caught even Dylan's fans off guard. Paul Williams, the critic who founded the influential music magazine *Crawdaddy* and has written extensively on Bob Dylan, wrote perceptively in a cover review at the time that Dylan sounded on *John Wesley Harding* like "...some guy who might in fact just be on the verge of inventing rock and roll in, say, 1954."

But even if *John Wesley Harding* possessed an almost eerie sense of being divorced from its time, some saw shadows of the zeitgeist moving through its quiet morality tales. Rock critic Jon Landau, also writing in *Crawdaddy,* believed that, in the album's lyrics, "Dylan manifests a profound awareness of the war and how it is affecting all of us." Whether or not this was actually the case, Landau's perspective is indicative of a reemerging

time when musicians—especially Dylan—were *expected* to have and offer their own point of view on external events.

As Landau noted in his *John Wesley Harding* review, Dylan had disdained the challenge posed by the work of other rock musicians. Dylan's album marks a break, if nothing else, and at the end of 1967, from the inward-looking nature of the important albums from the previous year or two—the evolutionary arc that is most simply described as beginning with the Beach Boys' *Pet Sounds,* peaking with *Sgt. Pepper,* and beginning its downward trajectory with the Rolling Stones' stilted *Their Satanic Majesty's Request.* Popular music began, in the main, to once again look outward and react to the world around it. And, as with Landau's take on Dylan

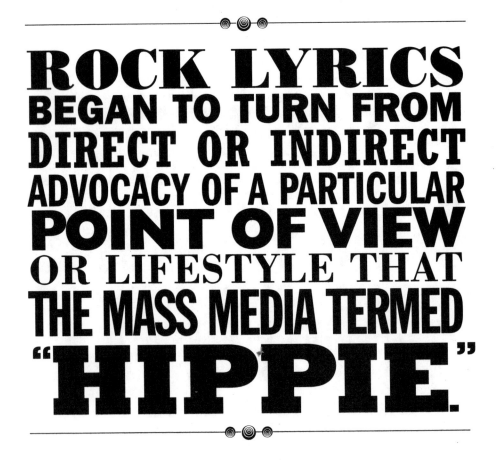

ROCK LYRICS
BEGAN TO TURN FROM DIRECT OR INDIRECT
ADVOCACY OF A PARTICULAR
POINT OF VIEW
OR LIFESTYLE THAT
THE MASS MEDIA TERMED
"HIPPIE."

reveals, even songs with no overt topical references couldn't help rubbing up against the whirlwind of current events.

Rock and roll had helped give birth to the 1960s counterculture and had played a huge role in informing and determining its values and its overall shape. By 1968, the vibe was not only in place but had come to permeate the mainstream. As Paul Kantner, guitarist for Jefferson Airplane, put it, "We went to, I think, Grinnell College in Iowa once, in 1967, and all the people came in to the show in, like, prom gowns and tuxedos and then we came back to Grinnell the next year and they were having, like, nude love-ins, and mud-bath parties, and acid freak-outs and all this sort of thing...in just one year." Or, as *Rolling Stone* correspondent P. J. O'Rourke somewhat more cynically puts it, 1968 was "the year that dope hit the hinterlands."

This even as the animating spark had begun to burn out. Near the end of 1967 the Diggers, a commune that among other things ran a "free store," staged a "Death of the Hippie" parade down San Francisco's Haight Street, the very cradle of the counterculture.

Bill Kreutzmann, the drummer for the Grateful Dead, marched carrying a cross to which, in a nod to psychedelic absurdity, a local sculptor had attached a water spigot.

Rock lyrics began to turn from direct or indirect advocacy of a particular point of view or lifestyle that the mass media, seizing on a Beat culture putdown, termed "hippie" (as Sam Andrew of Big Brother and the Holding Company recalls, "They would say, 'oh these people aren't hipsters, they're hippies'") to articulating that point of view's opposition to the headlines of the day. The relationship between music and the news of the day wasn't always precise or one way—as Andrew puts it, how the headlines "affected the music we were making...[is] hard to say...if there was a cause or effect relationship. I think that the entire society was entering this period of malaise." Whichever way the influence flowed, there was undeniable frisson between the turmoil of 1968 and an inspired and emotional period in rock and roll history.

And in 1968 the turmoil began with Vietnam.

CHAPTER ONE

THE TET OFFENSIVE

f you had to pick a single day as the turning point of the war that became America's most painful military defeat, it would have to be January 30, 1968: the day the Army of the Republic of Vietnam launched the Tet Offensive. This is how the year began.

The Vietnam War was an undeclared war, an American military intervention that had started in 1954 with just 400 military advisers. The former French colony in Southeast Asia had been split in two that year by treaty—in North Vietnam, the government was Communist; in the South, an American-backed dictatorship ruled. President Eisenhower had sent the advisers to train the South Vietnamese Army against the threat of invasion from the North and a growing insurrection in South Vietnam itself, known as the Viet Cong.

The United States feared that if South Vietnam fell, the rest of Southeast Asia—Laos, Cambodia, Thailand—would also fall, like dominoes, to Communism...and that India and the rest of Asia would ultimately topple as well.

But the Vietnamese people largely regarded it as their own civil war, a conflict that had pitted them first against the French colonial powers and then against a Western-backed dictatorship that had been forced upon them. By the early 1960s, the Viet Cong, with support from the Soviet Union and the People's Republic of China, were taking control of increasing areas of South Vietnam. A troubled President Kennedy sent ever-greater numbers of military advisers in response; by 1962 they numbered 11,000, though the official line was that they were noncombat troops.

At the time of Kennedy's assassination at the end of 1963, there were 23,000 American military advisers in Vietnam. When Vice President Lyndon Baines Johnson—LBJ—assumed the presidency, he retained the foreign policy team behind the military buildup half a world away, a group referred to with irony by writer and Vietnam war chronicler David Halberstam as "the best and the brightest." They were establishment men from the best families and the best schools. And they were sinking America deeper and deeper into a quagmire that would tear the country apart.

On August 7, 1964, the United States Congress responded to reports that North Vietnamese gunships had fired on American war-

ships off the Vietnamese coast by passing the Tonkin Gulf Resolution. In 1965, the first officially designated U.S. ground troops went to battle in South Vietnam. B-52 bombers dropped tons of bombs on North Vietnam. By the end of the year there were 180,000 American troops in Vietnam. What had begun as a training mission had become a deadly shooting war for the United States fighting force in Vietnam.

During 1966 and 1967, the war had escalated further and the American force had continued to grow. There were now more than half a million U.S. soldiers in the cities, hamlets, jungles, and mountains of this small Asian land, and in 1967 alone, nearly 10,000 of them came home in body bags.

By 1968, the war was going either swell or awful, depending on whom you believed. Every day army spokesmen gave the unvaryingly optimistic

line to an increasingly skeptical Saigon press corps in what had become known as the "Five O'Clock Follies." After every encounter with the Viet Cong, the army public relations specialists would report huge numbers of enemy dead and only a marginal number of American casualties. Why, then, had the enemy not been eradicated?

"They would tell you we lost twelve guys and the other side lost two thousand guys," remembers Creedence Clearwater Revival frontman John Fogerty, who spent two years in the Army reserves. "And soon it seemed like, well, the other guys have lost ten million guys, and we've lost thirty. And yet you're seeing these newsreels of devastation and our Army is being pushed back, and not doing very well."

The Vietnamese New Year, or Tet, fell on January 30, 1968. It had been customary for both sides to declare a truce on such holidays, and this Tet was no different. Despite intelligence reports showing an alarming buildup of VC soldiers and supplies throughout South Vietnam, the Americans didn't take any unusual actions.

Back in the states, MGM Records on that day released the Velvet Underground's second album, *White Light, White Heat.* The event went unmentioned by the CIA and military intelligence. Cause and effect cannot be proven, of course, but someone should have noticed.

On midnight of January 30, all hell broke loose in South Vietnam. Some 84,000 Viet Cong and North Vietnamese attacked thirty-six of forty-three provincial capitals in South Vietnam, five of six autonomous cities, and at least fifty hamlets. For the Communist forces, it was an assault of unprecedented force and range.

And never before had America's military machine seemed so impotent. The Viet Cong attacked the presidential palace and the government radio station in the South Vietnamese capital of Saigon. They even briefly breached the perimeter of the American Embassy compound while stunned Americans back home watched the drama on television. In the provincial capital of Hue, the Viet Cong launched an onslaught that would keep American troops under siege for thirty days.

"The Tet Offensive convinced me, although I was pretty well convinced already, but it started to convince the rest of America, that we were not

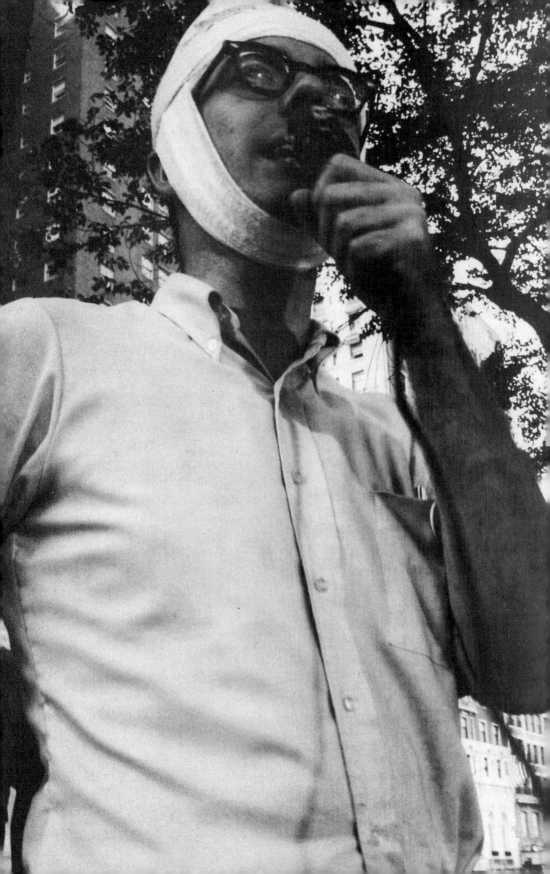

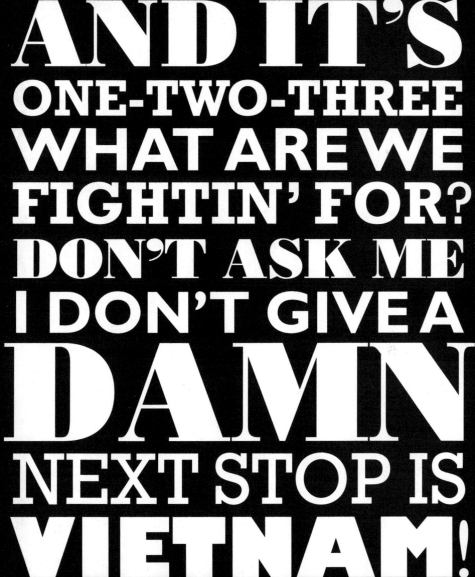

going to win," musician David Crosby said. "That we were being lied to. Here was supposedly, you know, a force whose body counts suddenly starts just kicking our butt all over Vietnam. Everywhere. Everybody on my end of things knew we shouldn't have been there. But now the whole country knew we were going to get our asses handed to us." Echoed writer P. J. O'Rourke, "The Tet Offensive was important because what sort of sunk in in the month or two or three that followed...was that we were not going to win that war in Vietnam."

The desperation of the effort to maintain order in the capital was conveyed by the summary public execution of a suspected Viet Cong by a Saigon policeman in front of press cameras. The act was captured on film and in still photographs. The image of the victim grimacing at the precise moment the bullet pierced his skull became an enduring symbol of a dark and murderous era.

The Viet Cong suffered enormous casualties. And their goal—that the Tet Offensive would launch a popular uprising that would end the war with their total victory—did not transpire. But they scored a huge psychological victory, and the war's momentum tilted in their favor. As Lance Morrow of *Time* magazine wrote, "Tet broke whatever residual spell was left in America's old Cold War calls to arms in the name of defending freedom around the globe. America's national morale curdled."

Walter Cronkite, the avuncular CBS News anchorman often called "the most trusted man in America," lost his cool when he heard about the Tet Offensive. "What the hell is going on?" he was heard to shout. "I thought we were winning this war."

If Cronkite, the distinguished voice of the media establishment, felt bewildered, he was not alone.

A rhetorical war raged at home, with "hawks" insisting we carry on with the war and "doves" demanding we declare peace and bring all our troops home. In 1968, after Tet, the war, in the eloquent words of *Newsday* reporter Fred Bruning, "split this country like an ax."

With the inverted logic that characterized the Vietnam War from its inception, the Viet Cong's battlefield "defeat" was a disaster for the American political and military establishment.

"Before the Tet Offensive the Vietnam War enjoys the support of the liberal establishment and it's being prosecuted by Lyndon Johnson," says historian Charles Kaiser. "Although he's unpopular in some quarters, virtually everybody in the beginning of 1968 thinks he is invulnerable and certain to be the Democratic nominee [for a second full term as president] in the fall."

A week after Tet started, a poll showed that for the first time, a majority of the American people believed we should get out—and stay out—of Vietnam.

Rock and roll was amplifying and even molding public opinion. The antiwar movement marched to the strains of artists such as Country Joe and the Fish. Country Joe McDonald, a Navy veteran, and his bandmates were associated with the hedonistic San Francisco acid rock scene, which was true to a point. But whereas the Grateful Dead and Jefferson Airplane quartered themselves in hippie culture's ground zero—San Francisco's Haight-Ashbury—Country Joe and the Fish were bivouacked on the other side of the Bay Bridge in Berkeley, birthplace of the 1960s' radical movement.

Country Joe and the Fish had established themselves during the 1967 Summer of Love with an appropriately trippy album titled *Electric Music*

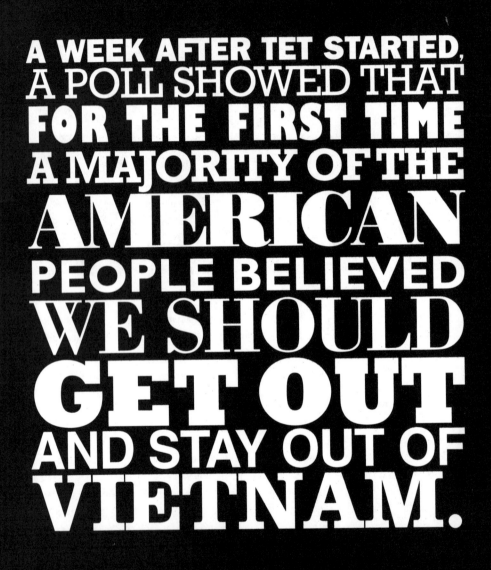

A WEEK AFTER TET STARTED, A POLL SHOWED THAT FOR THE FIRST TIME A MAJORITY OF THE AMERICAN PEOPLE BELIEVED WE SHOULD GET OUT AND STAY OUT OF VIETNAM.

for the *Mind and Body*. But in 1968, the group became famous for their darkly comic antiwar tune, "Fixin' to Die Rag":

> *And it's one-two-three*
> *What are we fightin' for?*
> *Don't ask me I don't give a damn*
> *Next stop is Vietnam!*

"To be perfectly blunt, the message of the song is, fuck you," McDonald says today, "Fuck you, Mr. President, fuck you, Department of Defense, fuck you, Commander in Chiefs. Fuck all you people. You want me to go out and die for something and you won't even explain it to me, you won't tell me what they did, so just fuck off."

The song resonated in the most unlikely of places. Phillip Butler, for eight years a prisoner of war (POW) in the "Hanoi Hilton," first heard the song played as propaganda by "Hanoi Hanna" on a Viet Cong radio program. He found it "compelling." He and his fellow POWs responded to its "great rhythm" and its "nice, black GI humor." Butler recalls "barefooted POWs kind of skipping around the room to, 'Altogether now, one, two, three, what

are we fighting for?/Whoopie, we're all gonna die' is pretty funny when you're sitting there in a situation like that. It rings very true for you."

Butler says now that "Music like Country Joe's helped us to stay sane. What little of it we could get, it was like a gem that came through from time to time." It's a sentiment shared by many who fought in Vietnam, where armed forces radio was tightly controlled but where GIs set up bandit radio stations in the field. Recalls Vietnam veteran Michael Kelly, "I just spun the dials...lo and behold there's Midnight Jack broadcasting: 'Midnight Jack, man, I'm deep in the jungle. Oh, bad news, my man,' he says. 'What can I play for you man? How about some Jimi Hendrix?' He's gone for about 30 seconds and I imagine he's putting a reel-to-reel tape on, y'know, and here comes Jimi Hendrix..."

Hendrix's music, especially his definitive cover of Bob Dylan's "All Along the Watchtower" (from *John Wesley Harding*) with its opening lines of "There must be some kinda way outta here..." was, for Vietnam veterans, part of the soundtrack to the war. The Doors, too, were a big part of this

musical collage; their haunting, otherworldly music seemed to capture the tension and fear they were feeling. Their 1968 album *Waiting for the Sun* carried an explicit commentary on the war, "The Unknown Soldier": "Breakfast where the news is read/television, children fed/unborn living, living dead/bullet strikes the helmet's head...." For troops in the jungles of Southeast Asia, songs like this brought things full circle—they were listening to a musical report of how the way they were fighting was being received back home.

Michael Kelly also remembers that "the number one anthem of all the troops when I was there was Eric Burdon and the Animals' 'We Gotta Get Out of This Place.' Anytime that we were in the rear and that song was played or it came on, everyone would stop, everyone would join in at the top of their lungs—it was just the best, best song."

On the political front, Vietnam's civil war was becoming America's civil crisis. Liberal Democrats against the war challenged Lyndon Johnson for the party's presidential nomination. Two men in particular, antiwar activists Allard Lowenstein and Curtis Gans, led the initiative. As Charles Kaiser puts it, they had "gone around to every Democratic senator, liberal senator, antiwar senator starting with Bobby Kennedy and they've begged each of them to run for president to challenge Lyndon Johnson and each of them in turn has refused until they reach Eugene McCarthy."

McCarthy was, according to Kaiser, "like Bob Dylan, a poet from Minnesota with somewhat mystical tendencies." A stretch perhaps, but not an absurd one. McCarthy was a professorial type who disdained politics, a remarkably aloof and distant man who in a few short months turned conventional political wisdom on its head. He entered the New Hampshire presidential primary—the first by tradition, and therefore crucial—and came in a very strong second to incumbent LBJ.

President Johnson had the support of every elected official in New Hampshire. But across the country, even downright respectable members of the party's establishment were speaking out firmly against the war. Democratic Senator Frank Church of Idaho, who served on the powerful Senate Foreign Relations committee, called for an "agonizing reappraisal" of America's policy, and flatly stated that the U.S. goal of stabilizing that part of Asia was "a grandiose dream of men who suffer from the dangerous illusion of American omnipotence."

Johnson barely won in New Hampshire despite being the well-funded choice of the party establishment. New Hampshire was, then as now, an essentially conservative state, and McCarthy was no firebrand as a campaigner. "A terrible speaker," as historian Kaiser recalls.

Writing in *The Village Voice*, the liberal Kennedy friend Jack Newfield called McCarthy's speeches "Dull, vague, and without either balls or poetry." And he summed up with the wish of many when he said: "Make Bobby Kennedy run."

But Robert F. Kennedy was deeply torn. There had been bad blood, guilt, and ambivalence between President Johnson and the Kennedys ever since Johnson was sworn in on November 22, 1963, over John F. Kennedy's dead body. And many Democrats yearned for a return to the Camelot of the Kennedy years—they felt it was manifest destiny that JFK's younger brother Robert would be president. RFK, who had been attorney general under his brother, and was in 1968 a U.S. senator from New York, never denied his hunger for the White House...but when would he run?

Robert Kennedy was still on the political sidelines while McCarthy's reputation for ineffectiveness was spreading even among his supporters. The White House, meanwhile, approached the New Hampshire primary with undisguised arrogance. John Bailey, the chairman of the Democratic National Committee, even refused to allow McCarthy to discuss the opposition to Vietnam at a January 7, 1968, convention planning session. "The Democratic National Convention is as good as over," Bailey said. "It will be Lyndon Johnson again, and that's that." Famous last words.

Against this backdrop, the thousands of young college students who campaigned for McCarthy in the New Hampshire primary seemed on a fool's errand. "The polls continued to say that the senator from Minnesota had no chance to upset

"ACCORDINGLY, I SHALL NOT SEEK, AND I WILL NOT ACCEPT, THE NOMINATION OF MY PARTY FOR ANOTHER TERM AS YOUR PRESIDENT."

an incumbent president," historian Jules Witcover wrote in his book *1968: The Year the Dream Died.* "But college students by the carload streaming into the state on weekends and many checking out of college for the duration of the primary, generated an almost joyful optimism in the ranks."

By mid-February, the McCarthy campaign was "a veritable army...working in church basements and sleeping in private homes, sometimes in beds, sometimes in sleeping bags on floors." From colleges in the Northeast and even as faraway as the Midwest, young men and women crisscrossed the Granite State in the cold.

By March 12, 1968, the day of the primary, McCarthy's youth army had convinced a sizable percentage of New Hampshire's skeptical Democratic voters. Despite a fierce snowstorm, the young volunteers continued to work throughout the day, even driving voters to the polls. When the votes were tallied that night, LBJ had won 49.4 percent of the

Democratic vote, McCarthy 42.2 percent. With write-in votes from those voting in the Republican primary, according to Jules Witcover, McCarthy garnered just 230 fewer votes than the president of the United States.

The results were not unlike those of the Tet. True, LBJ had won more votes. But McCarthy's strength showed the president's vulnerability and marked a turning point in public perception. "Soon after the polls closed," Witcover wrote, "it was clear that they had pulled off a political upset of immense proportions."

The taste of victory for McCarthy, though sweet, did not linger. Once Bobby Kennedy saw that Johnson was vulnerable, he told Sam Donaldson of ABC News that "I am actively reconsidering" entering the Democratic primary race. He told a syndicated Washington newspaper reporter that "the divisions of the Democratic party are already there, and I can't be blamed for creating them."

McCarthy was bitter: "He wouldn't even let me have my day of celebration, would he?" On March 16, Kennedy formally announced his candidacy.

The battleground shifted to other primary states, such as Wisconsin and even Kennedy's native Massachusetts, where he had entered too late to be on the ballot. McCarthy supporters saw Kennedy as a spoiler; but Kennedy's supporters felt that McCarthy could not win in the November election. Committed antiwar Democrats agonized over whom to back, or work for. It was hard to stay focused on the goal of defeating Lyndon Johnson's renomination as presidential candidate of the party...and the ultimate goal of winning the general election in the fall.

But on the evening of March 31, President Johnson appeared on national television. He delivered a forty-minute speech in which he talked of a limited reduction in the bombing of North Vietnam and a modest increase, 13,500, in troops

sent there. (General Westmoreland had asked for more than 200,000 soldiers). Near the end of the speech, having become convinced that no one would take his desire for peace seriously as long as his political career was on the line, Johnson made the announcement that stunned the country, and the world. "Accordingly, I shall not seek, and I will not accept, the nomination of my party for another term as your president."

McCarthy's "children's crusade," whose goal had been considered a pipe dream just two months earlier, had triumphed beyond its wildest expectations. The end of the war seemed in sight. For a brief period much of America dared to exhale. On the radio, Otis Redding's posthumous master-piece "(Sittin' On) The Dock of the Bay" provided a mellow accompaniment to what was, in retrospect, a lull in the storm. The good feelings would last exactly five days.

1968

CHAPTER TWO

THE
KING
IS DEAD

o most black Americans, 1967's Summer of Love may as well have taken place on Mars. While white kids wore flowers in their hair, waved peace signs, and sang along to Sgt. Pepper's Lonely Hearts Club Band, *black America seethed with long-denied demands for true justice and equality.*

"GOD...ALLOWED ME TO GO UP TO THE MOUNTAIN, AND I'VE LOOKED OVER, AND SEEN THE PROMISED LAND. I MAY NOT GET THERE WITH YOU. BUT I WANT YOU TO KNOW THAT WE, AS A PEOPLE, WILL GET TO THE PROMISED LAND... I'M NOT FEARING ANY MAN. MINE EYES HAVE SEEN THE GLORY OF THE COMING OF THE LORD."

A buoyant American economy had passed blacks by. During the previous ten years, whites had left the cities in a mass exodus to the suburbs. In many ways, the cities of Detroit and Newark were typical of the abandonment of black America.

The need for labor in the automotive plants of Detroit and manufacturing jobs in the factories in and around Newark had drawn hundreds of thousands of blacks fleeing poverty and discrimination in the South. Although blacks had the most dangerous and unappealing jobs, there was plenty of work to go around. During the 1950s, however, automation of the auto factories caused many of these semiskilled and unskilled jobs to disappear.

At the same time, Detroit was like many other American cities in its de facto segregation.

Discriminatory real estate practices, bank-lending policies, "gentlemen's agreements," and outright intimidation from white citizens and law enforcement forced blacks into inner-city ghettos. There they were victimized by absentee landlords who charged relatively high prices for poor housing; even when they owned their own homes, blacks were denied the access to capital that would have enabled them to make improvements. And so the ghettoes went from bad to worse.

As the sixties progressed, the dearth of decent housing, the evaporation of factory jobs, and staggering rates of unemployment among blacks caused frustration and anger to boil over.

Uprisings in New York's Harlem in 1964, and Los Angeles's Watts in 1965, helped set the stage for what author James Baldwin had prophetically called "The Fire Next Time."

On July 13, a Newark cab driver named John Smith was stopped for tailgating a police car and

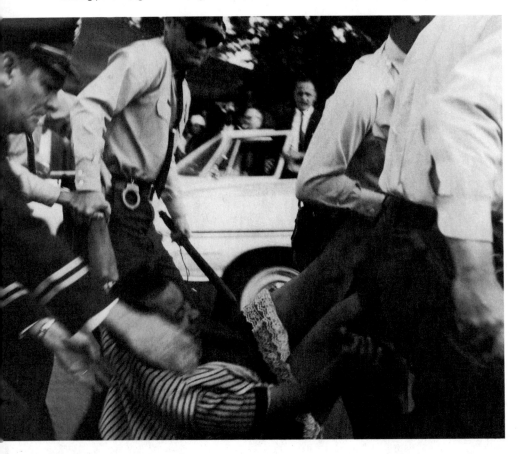

other vehicle infractions. Newark, with a population then of 400,000, had a black majority. Its 1,400 member police force had 250 blacks, none in ranks of responsibility.

In the ensuing heated disagreement, Smith was subdued with what police called "necessary force." Smith needed hospitalization. A crowd surged around the police station, threw molotov cocktails, and then all hell broke loose. When the riot ended four days later, 26 people were dead, more than 1,500 injured, and another 1,000 arrested. The entire downtown was razed by fire.

Less than a week after the riot in Newark, Detroit was in flames. It started on July 23, 1967, when police raided a black after-hours club. Friction between police and blacks in Detroit was nothing new, and after a scuffle, the police withdrew.

But the tinderbox had been ignited. And this time the conflagration didn't stop until almost the entire downtown area was destroyed. The National Guard was called in to quell the riot, but it took an entire week. The toll: more than 40 dead, 14 square miles burned to the ground, 2,000 arrested and more than 5,000 left homeless, almost all black, by the indiscriminate torching.

The flames spread with varying intensity throughout the country: there were nearly fifty riots

that could be described as racial in the summer of 1967. Aretha Franklin's electrifying cover of Otis Redding's "Respect" blasted from car radios and jukeboxes that summer, but it was almost too late for that: Black America was lashing out in anger over wrongs past and present in a paroxysm of R-E-V-E-N-G-E.

After the Watts riots two years earlier, President Johnson had appointed a commission, headed by former Illinois Governor Otto Kerner, to examine the causes of racial unrest in America. The National Advisory Commission on Civil Disorders, known as the Kerner Report, was delivered on March 1, 1968. It concluded that despite the passage of Civil Rights laws the country was "moving toward two separate and unequal societies, one black, one white."

The Kerner Commission squarely blamed white racism as the root cause. Though many fair-minded people might have agreed, the Kerner Report generated a white backlash. Fearful of the lawlessness on TV each day, many whites ceased to sympathize with black Americans and their litany of injustices that dated back to slavery.

A writer for *First Things*, a publication of the Conservative Institute on Religion and Public Life, boldly stated that, "Most white Americans rejected the claim that they were incorrigible racists and so

IT WAS KING'S COMMITMENT TO NONVIOLENT PROTEST THAT HAD GIVEN THE CIVIL RIGHTS MOVEMENT ITS UNDENIABLE UNDERPINNING OF RIGHTEOUSNESS AND HAD CONVINCED SO MANY WHITE AMERICANS THAT THE CAUSE OF EQUAL RIGHTS FOR THE BLACK MINORITY WAS A MORAL IMPERATIVE.

simply shrugged off the Kerner Commission's indulgent exercise in guilt mongering."

Alabama Governor George C. Wallace sought to take advantage of white resentment. He decided that the time was right for a serious run at the presidency.

Wallace's run would change the arithmetic of American politics. Alabama, like the rest of the Deep South, had been loyally Democratic ever since the Civil War and a certain Republican named Abraham Lincoln. In national elections, the Democrats could count on a nearly unbroken bloc of electoral votes from the Carolinas to Louisiana. When Wallace left the Democrats in 1968, he took that Southern bloc with him forever. The electoral landslides of Richard Nixon in 1972 and Ronald Reagan in 1980 and 1984 were constructed on solid Republican sweeps of the once-Democratic South.

The Kerner Report didn't tell most blacks anything they didn't already know. Few were surprised by the report's implication that white racism was too deeply ingrained to ever willingly accommodate the aspirations of the black community.

In February 1968, the book *Soul on Ice* was published. Its author was Eldridge Cleaver, an ex-convict who had done prison time for rape. (*Soul on Ice* provocatively suggested that raping white women was a revolutionary political act.) Cleaver was intense, handsome, and articulate, angry as hell, and with guns loaded.

He was also the Minister of Information for the Black Panther Party, a political/social/paramilitary organization based in Oakland, California. The group believed in self-determination and self-defense for blacks. They armed themselves and insisted that, if attacked by the police, they would shoot back.

Cleaver argued that black neighborhoods in American cities were under enemy occupation—the metro police—in much the way Vietnamese cities were by American soldiers. "The police do on the domestic level what the armed forces do on the international level: Protect the way of life of those in power," Cleaver wrote.

Noting with pride the Watts uprising of 1965, he stated, "Blacks are looking on and asking tactical questions. They are asked to die for the System in Vietnam. In Watts, they are killed by it. Now—*Now!*—they are asking each other in dead earnest: Why not die right here in Babylon fighting for a better life, like the Viet Cong? If those little cats can do it, what's wrong with big studs like us?"

Such rhetoric wore heavily on Martin Luther King Jr. It was King's commitment to nonviolent protest that had given the Civil Rights movement its undeniable underpinning of righteousness and had convinced so many white Americans that the cause of equal rights for the black minority was a moral imperative. And as King himself exhorted his black followers, "Let us learn to turn the other cheek with the realization that it is better to go through life with a scarred-up body than with a scarred-up soul."

In 1963, his "I Have a Dream Speech" made King a figure of historic, international stature comparable to that of his hero, Mahatma Gandhi. In 1964, he won the Nobel Peace Prize. In 1965, the brutal, televised attack of peaceful marchers by racist Southern law officers in Selma, Alabama, outraged people of goodwill everywhere. President Johnson had been able to channel that outrage into the overwhelming passage of the Voting Rights Act, which helped end hundreds of years of black disenfranchisement in the South. It also drove Southern racists like George Wallace from the Democratic fold forever.

The charismatic King had powerful enemies. On one end was the paranoid FBI director J. Edgar Hoover, who thought King a traitor, a Communist, and worse. Hoover kept him under constant surveillance and even blackmailed King by taking secret photographs of his sexual indiscretions. Hoover, the most powerful law-enforcement official in America, called King a "degenerate."

On the other end of the spectrum the increasingly militant black power movement thought King's commitment to integration through pacifism passé: too little, too late. The Student Non-Violent Coordinating Committee, or SNCC, began to ignore the "nonviolent" part of its name under fiery leaders such as Stokely Carmichael (who coined the phrase "black power") and H. Rap Brown (who after the 1967 riots observed that "violence is as American as cherry pie"). Many white liberals were frustrated at being excluded, while a large number of blue-collar whites were simply enraged by such rhetoric.

Such were the divisions precipitated by and within the Civil Rights movement. But by 1968 they had still not come to a head. The passage of Civil Rights laws in the mid-1960s had inspired some sense of progress, even if it was a long time coming and was, for many, moving far too slowly.

Pop music had brought the spirit of the movement and of black pride to the radio dial—to a greater degree than it had ever been before, or has been since. Many formerly all-white radio stations had begun to play black artists as well, phasing out the days when R&B and soul were considered "race music." Motown Records, under entrepreneur Berry Gordy Jr., had become the most successful black-owned business in the country. The appeal of the label's polished, stage-savvy performers (which included Diana Ross's Supremes, the Temptations, the Miracles with Smokey Robinson, the Four Tops, Martha and the Vandellas, Stevie Wonder, Marvin Gaye, and others) was underlined by Motown's slogan: "The Sound of Young America."

Motown got white and black youths dancing to the same beat and opened the door for other black artists and other labels: the electrifying James Brown; the urbane and aggressive Wilson Pickett; the peerless, gospel-trained Aretha Franklin; the smooth, eloquent Otis Redding. Integrated studio groups like Booker T & the MGs also helped make the mid-1960s a time of racial harmony on record, if not in the society at large.

During the early 1960s, artists like Curtis Mayfield and his group the Impressions were right in the middle. The Chicago vocal group's updated gospel songs—"Amen," "Keep on Pushin'," "I'm So Proud," "People Get Ready"—became the sound-track of the Civil Rights movement.

In 1968, Mayfield's big crossover hit was "We're a Winner," a song that articulated both feelings of black pride and the sense that progress was being and had been made on the Civil Rights front. As the late Mayfield remembered years later, "Black folks needed to hear that and it helped, in its own way, I suppose, with the struggle...and it wasn't even so much the depth of lyric but, 'we're movin' on up, Lord have mercy, we're movin' up.'"

"To many young people coming of age in the 1960s," Charles Kaiser wrote, "this combination of integrated audiences worshiping black music and integrated crowds cheering [Martin Luther] King's rhetoric made it look as if cultural and political gaps between the races might disappear in their lifetimes."

But for the typical black citizen living in places like Memphis—home of Stax/Volt Records, the label of Otis Redding, Booker T & the MGs, Rufus and Carla Thomas, and many other soul stars—and Motown's Detroit, progress on radio playlists made no measurable difference in their plight. In March 1968, Memphis's mostly black sanitation workers went on strike, seeking to unionize.

During that month, King led a march that turned into a violent encounter with police, leaving one protester dead, 60 injured, and 200 arrested.

King was said to be deeply depressed. "Maybe we just have to admit that the day of violence is here...maybe we just have to give up, and let violence take its course," he told stunned associates.

King made one of his most memorable and impassioned speeches in Memphis on April 3, 1968. He seemed at peace with the struggle and with the possibility of his own death: "God...allowed me to go up to the mountain, and I've looked over, and seen the promised land. I may not get there with you. But I want you to know that we, as a people, will get to the promised land...I'm not fearing any man. Mine eyes have seen the glory of the coming of the Lord."

His words proved prophetic. The next afternoon a shot rang out as King stepped out onto the balcony of his Memphis motel room. Dr. Martin Luther King Jr. fell, killed by an assassin's bullet. It seemed at the time as if the dream of racial harmony died with him.

A white man named James Earl Ray was arrested and convicted of King's killing. But doubts have plagued the case since his arrest. And at the time of Ray's death in prison in 1998, there was still so much about the case that didn't add up that even King's widow and children doubted that Ray killed King; they felt that he was set up to take the fall by unrevealed conspirators.

Whoever killed King, whether Ray or others, did not just kill a black leader. They killed, for a while, the country's hope, for at a time when America was coming apart at the seams, King seemed to be one of the few public figures with an interest in bringing people together. When the bullet felled King in Memphis, it was as if a bell had sounded and tens of thousands of people took to the streets in a spontaneous show of rage.

The deadly, devastating Newark and Detroit riots of the previous summer seemed like a dress rehearsal for what happened in the immediate aftermath of King's murder. Riots erupted in cities from coast to coast. The worst was in Washington, D.C., where some of the nation's toughest ghettos were just blocks away from the center of government. The nation shuddered at the sight of machine-gun nests at the Capitol and armed troops in defensive positions on the White House lawn.

James Brown, the Godfather of Soul, then in the prime of his popularity as both a performer and symbol of black self-respect, was scheduled to do a concert in Boston that night. With the city's black community set to explode, Brown did a remarkable thing: He went on local television and gave a concert that kept many potential rioters and looters off the streets, got them to cool down, to think.

"It was the only thing left to do, somebody getting in their right mind," Brown said. When the crowd at the concert seemed on the verge of rioting, Brown urged restraint. As people began to clash in the aisles and storm the stage, Brown stood at the microphone and implored, "Wait a minute...wait! This is no way—we are black! We are black! Now, wait a minute...I asked the police to step back because I figured I could get some respect from my own people. Now are we together, we?"

When the answer came back from the crowd as a ringing affirmative, Brown proceeded to perform one of the most emotional shows of his career.

Brown is a complicated man, a former dirt-poor shoeshine boy from Augusta, Georgia, whose show business success gave him a strong faith in the power of economic self-determination.

Asked at the time how he defined Black Power, Brown answered, "Get Green Power. Black Pride. There's a difference between pride and power. Your power's in your thinking."

Brown communicated many of those thoughts in his songs. Between August 1967 and the end of 1968, Brown had eight hits in the top 40. Many were sex-infused funk workouts, such as

SAY IT LOUD: I'M BLACK AND I'M PROUD!

MOTOWN
GOT WHITE AND BLACK YOUTHS
DANCING
TO THE SAME BEAT
AND OPENED THE
DOOR FOR OTHER
BLACK ARTISTS.

"Cold Sweat," "I Got the Feeling," and "Licking Stick." But others, like "There Was a Time" and "Get It Together," hinted at larger topics. None, though, had the impact of "Say It Loud, I'm Black and I'm Proud."

"You call someone that and you had a problem," Brown said, meaning the word "black." "He wasn't proud of his color. And beauty's only skin deep, so just go skin deep, and get the beauty...I'm glad I was able to do some good...all of us should be proud."

As music journalist Tim White puts it, "'Say It Loud, I'm Black and I'm Proud' was like, let's skip the preliminaries, let's get to the main event...it was anthem as personal explosion." When the song was first released, he remembers, "It came out of the dashboard of your car and it put a new part in your hair." Such was its directness, and its effect on the awareness of listeners, black and white.

James Brown was not the only black artist to respond musically to the King assassination. Aretha Franklin, whose father was a well-known black preacher, released her anthemic "Think" in the wake of the tragedy. Like Brown's onstage call to peace in Boston, "Think" urges reflection—and holds out the promise in its ringing middle eight of "freedom, freedom, freedom," in an echo and affirmation of Martin Luther King's famous "free at last" refrain.

"You have to stand up and be counted for things that you believe in and what you feel is right. And that's what I did," Franklin says today.

King's assassination branded the American psyche. If you were alive on that day in 1968, you remember where you were when you heard the news in the same way that people can tell you what they were doing when they heard that JFK had been shot or when man first walked on the moon.

Big Brother and the Holding Company was sharing a bill with blues legend B. B. King that night at Generation, a club owned by Jimi Hendrix in New York City. Sam Andrew of Big Brother remembers that night as "scary...kind of like the Cuban missile crisis"—a night where the violence of King's shooting and the fury of the riots had brought America to a crossroads and "it could have gone either way."

Andrew remembers that B. B. King talked about the assassination for a time backstage. "King was so noble and articulate about it," he recalls, "and then he went out and did his set. It was like church...sanctified...the feeling that he put out and the understanding and the harmony."

Dave Getz, drummer for Big Brother, was also in the room when the band and B. B. King found out that King had been killed. He remembers B. B. King as showing the sort of grace and dignity in the situation for which people knew the other King. Getz remembers that the blues guitarist was "not filled with rage, though I'm sure there was a lot of emotion." Getz, too, remembers the empathy between him and the audience. "It was an incredible night," he says.

In a year when—as journalist Tim White puts it—"There were so many divisions...you couldn't even add them up," April 4 moved the country from fractured to shattered.

"YOU HAVE TO STAND UP AND BE COUNTED FOR THINGS THAT YOU BELIEVE IN AND WHAT YOU FEEL IS RIGHT."

CHAPTER THREE

REVOLT!

he United States was not the only Western nation divided against itself in 1968: The whole world seemed on the verge of, as the Rolling Stones' "Street Fighting Man" put it that year, "violent revolution." America roiled with protest over the Vietnam War and in the wake of the King assassination, Europe was swept up by the most serious wave of social unrest in more than a century. "There have been two worldwide revolutions—one took place in 1848 and the other in 1968," a Czech professor has written. "Both of them foundered. Both of them changed the world." And Czechoslovakia indeed saw revolution in 1968—and saw it crushed by Soviet tanks.

"THE THING THAT I HATED MOST ABOUT THE WAR IN VIETNAM, IF I AM TO BE HONEST, WAS THE PROSPECT OF BEING DRAFTED."

In West Germany, the attempted assassination of socialist leader "Red" Rudi Dutschke on April 11 provoked a wave of protests and violence that left two dead and scores injured and arrested.

In France, students rioted in the spring against the inequalities they saw in their educational system and, by extension, their government. The war in Vietnam, which had begun as a revolution against the French colonial government, also touched off widespread student demonstrations at home.

Though young American radicals, like their counterparts in France and elsewhere in Europe, gave lip service to the notion of solidarity with the working class, circumstances in the United States made such a coupling unlikely. For one thing, employment was high and income good for

white blue-collar workers in 1968, who had little trouble meeting mortgage payments on suburban homes and maintaining two cars in the garage. They were living what they regarded as the American Dream, and they largely regarded anti-war protesters as spoiled college kids and the counterculture—popular musicians and their fans included—likewise.

This perception was, to a degree and at times, accurate. As Grace Slick, lead singer of Jefferson Airplane (and later Starship) recalls, "You [did] care about how the country's going and about how the world's going, but I would have to say there was an awful lot of 'what's in it for me?'"

Or as journalist P. J. O'Rourke flatly puts it, "The thing that I hated most about the war in

Vietnam, if I'm to be honest, was the prospect of being drafted."

Indeed, the class division was evident among those who served and those who avoided serving in Vietnam. Though all young men between the ages of eighteen and twenty-five were obligated to register for the draft, college students received automatic draft deferments. As a result, those sent to fight were disproportionately poor—white, black, and Hispanic.

"It was very much as though the sergeant had come up to the front of the group and said, "'Everybody whose dad made more than twenty thousand dollars a year and has been to college, get over here, you're out,'" quips O'Rourke. "'Everybody whose dad made less than twenty

thousand a year or who didn't go to college, over here, you're in.'"

John Fogerty was trying to get his band, Creedence Clearwater Revival, off the ground when he joined the Army Reserves to avoid being drafted. He remembers being terrified before his draft physical: "It was like a series of events that would all come true in my mind—I'll be drafted, I'll most certainly go in the Army, I'll most certainly be sent to Vietnam, and I will most certainly go to Vietnam. That was the only scenario I could envision. So I set about immediately trying to figure out other avenues."

The evident inequality of the draft inspired Fogerty to pen one of CCR's best known songs, "Fortunate Son," released in 1968. As he recalls,

"OUR YOUNG PEOPLE IN DISTURBING NUMBERS APPEAR TO REJECT ALL FORMS OF AUTHORITY."

on a generation of young working-class men in America—not to mention upon the people of Vietnam.

America's college campuses were nonetheless alive with protest, which for many was in earnest struggle against the status quo. Perhaps at no time was the gap between American college students and authority dramatized more vividly than at Columbia University, the elite Ivy League college in New York City, during April 1968.

Student rebels cited many reasons for seizing the Columbia campus. Antiwar students objected to the university's cooperation with the Institute for Defense Analysis, a focal point for the contempt many students felt for anything connected to the military and the war.

Another issue was the university's plan for expansion in the area around its campus in Morningside Heights, in the predominantly black neighborhood of Harlem. Activist members of the Students for a Democratic Society (SDS) and the Students African-American Society (SAS) led protests objecting to the building of a Columbia gymnasium in the area, which would dislocate residents and raze an area then used for community recreation.

Fronted by campus SDS leader Mark Rudd and SAS leader Cicero Wilson, protesters seized Hamilton Hall, a main classroom building, and detained a college dean. Both Rudd and Wilson seemed to be suggesting a turning point in American protest, from nonviolent speech to violent confrontation.

The rhetoric alone was escalating almost out of control. "Wilson raised the specter of blacks on campus joining forces with Harlem residents to block the new building, violently if necessary," historian Jules Witcover writes. "Warning of another long hot summer of revolt and rioting, he asked the crowd...'Do you think this white citadel of hypocrisy will be bypassed if an insurrection occurs this summer?'"

Columbia President Grayson Kirk, a sixty-four-year-old WASP, was the perfect public foil for

"We have another system in America [that] really seems to come to the fore under times of crisis, like a big war...suddenly all the sons of rich guys don't have to go anywhere dangerous. That was really on my mind, I think, for several months when one day I got...the idea of a 'fortunate son'—sort of a twist on the phrase 'favorite son.' I don't know how I went from one to the other, but once I thought in terms of a fortunate son, all my venom came out."

The incisive social commentary of the song's lyric and the passionate performance on the recording made it a rallying point for those who saw the deadly injustice being perpetrated

such inflammatory rhetoric. He appeared unapologetically square, condescending, and out of touch.

"Our young people in disturbing numbers appear to reject all forms of authority," said Kirk in an April 12 speech, "and they have taken refuge in a turbulent and inchaote nihilism whose sole objectives are destructive. I know of no time in our history when the gap between the generations has been wider or more potentially dangerous."

Kirk's rigid posturing was positively inspirational to rebel leader Rudd. Quoting the black liberation poet LeRoi Jones (later known as Amiri Baraka), Rudd's reply was: "Up against the wall, motherfucker, this is a stick-up." Those words—or at least, the first four—became a rallying cry that would be heard on the streets, at the barricades, and in the title song of the Jefferson Airplane album *Volunteers*. As summed up by Airplane's Paul Kantner, the song captures well the radical mood of the time: "Attack the people who need to be attacked. But in a way that you can be effective and kick some ass."

Soon students had taken over five main buildings on the Columbia campus. This was no peaceful sit-in but an edgy, emotionally charged weeklong declaration of war. Kirk had had enough. He asked police to remove the protesters, resulting in one of the most violent clashes ever on an American campus. But similar, if not as violent, confrontations were taking place on college and university campuses across the country.

H. Rap Brown's words that "violence is as American as cherry pie" were taking on exceptional resonance. A few months earlier, in February, students at all-black South Carolina State College in Orangeburg attempted to integrate a bowling alley. State police and the National Guard responded with an unprovoked barrage of bullets. Three students were killed and thirty-four wounded. Police charged that students had opened fire first

but no one in the crowd saw any weapons, and none were ever found.

Historian Charles Kaiser was a high school senior about to enter Columbia when the April 1968 protests turned ugly. "The Columbia riots were even more baffling to traditional Americans than the black riots," says Kaiser. "After all, at least if you were living in a ghetto and had a terrible place to live and not enough food, there was some sort of rational explanation for why people were revolting against authority, whereas at Columbia, these were the children of the most privileged classes in America, and they were revolting against the system. And this was much more terrifying, in a way, to white middle-class America, to see people just like themselves fighting with the police."

While some members of the American middle class were once again turned off by violence perpetrated by the police, a majority still identified with the authorities. And even members of the minority groups embraced by the protesters were appalled.

"Looking at the world from a working-class neighborhood, looking at the takeover of Columbia University, people in my apartment building didn't go to Columbia, and people we knew didn't go to Columbia," recalled National Public Radio commentator Ray Suarez. "There was a feeling that this wasn't throwing off the shackles of an oppressive and airless society. It was people who were lucky, flaunting their luck, and you know, when you turned on the television and saw them dancing in a park in San Francisco while everybody you could see in the living room was tired from working all day. ...There was an irritation that didn't go to that second level of analysis where you say, well, what is it exactly that they are for or against? It was just, look at all these people who don't have to work their butt off like everybody I know does."

That feeling did not go unnoticed by Richard Nixon. Vice president from 1952 to 1960 under war hero Dwight D. "Ike" Eisenhower, Nixon had suffered seemingly career-ending defeats in the 1960 presidential election (to John F. Kennedy), and in the 1962 California governor's race, after which he self-pityingly told the press: "You won't have Richard Nixon to kick around anymore."

But after Republican Senator Barry Goldwater of Arizona lost the 1964 election by a landslide to President Johnson, the party was a shambles. Nixon worked masterfully behind the scenes to help it back on its feet. He knocked out early favorites like Michigan Governor George Romney and, benefiting from the indecision of New York Governor Nelson Rockefeller, marched through the 1968 Republican presidential primaries. The student demonstrators who loathed him would give him the issue he'd ride to victory in November:

law and order. He appealed to the fears of working- and middle-class Americans who watched the student protesters with anger and bewilderment. They were, in Nixon's coinage, the Silent Majority.

While an alliance between students and workers in the United States remained an impossible dream, France was a different story in 1968. With both students and workers angry at the passive condescension of an unresponsive and bloated government bureaucracy, both groups banded together to stage a general strike.

It began with 23,000 workers striking in 1967 in the French city of Lyon and grew to consume the entire nation. By May 1968, student boldness, worker rage, and brutal police overreaction had nearly brought down the government of Charles de Gaulle. Student demonstrations in Paris that month grew until anxious police attacked. Fighting spread. The Sorbonne,

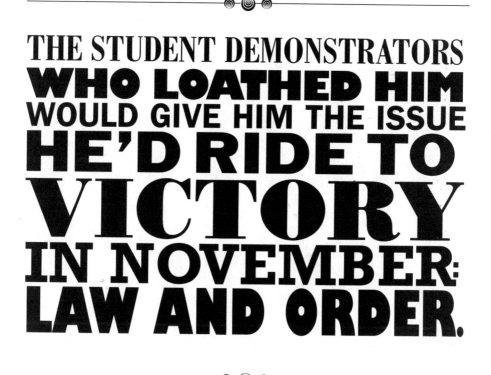

THE STUDENT DEMONSTRATORS WHO LOATHED HIM WOULD GIVE HIM THE ISSUE HE'D RIDE TO VICTORY IN NOVEMBER: LAW AND ORDER.

France's premier university, closed for only the second time in its 700-year history, the other time having been when the Nazis seized Paris in World War II.

May 6 was known as Bloody Monday. Students marching through Paris were again attacked by police. Students tore up paving stones and overturned cars to form barricades. Police pumped tear gas into the air and called for reinforcements. The Boulevard St. Germain became a bloody battleground. Official tally: 422 arrested, 345 policeman injured, untold number of demonstrators hurt.

The savagery of the police turned public opinion quickly to the students' side. The middle class were sickened by the police riot; the working class seemed buoyed by the students' courage. The crescendo rose as France spun out of control. Hundreds of thousands of students and workers fought and marched in the barricaded streets of Paris. Workers throughout the country went on strike and occupied their plants. France literally came to a standstill as air traffic controllers and mass transit, rail, and shipyard workers striked. They were joined by teachers and radio and television employees. Tourists were evacuated and the country was on the brink of revolution.

On May 24, President de Gaulle's televised appeal for reconciliation finally began to break striker unity. With an offer of a 35 percent increase in the minimum wage and an immediate 10 percent wage increase, France slowly drifted back to normal.

There was also protest across the Channel in England, though it was not nearly as widespread nor as impactful. It was nevertheless very real and the target was, at times, U.S. foreign policy as embodied by Vietnam and the English government's tacit support thereof.

Mick Jagger of the Rolling Stones was at a number of rallies in London in 1968, including an antiwar rally at the U.S. embassy. These events and the unrest around the world lent inspiration to the first single on their album *Beggars Banquet*, released later that year.

"Everywhere I hear the sound of marching, charging feet," sang Jagger. But then came what some saw as a hedge: "But what can a poor boy do/but to sing for a rock and roll band?/There's just no place for a street fightin' man."

If radicals were disappointed with the Stones' fudge on "Street Fighting Man," they would be incensed by a song that the Beatles wrote during and about the Paris riots, "Revolution."

"The immediate inspiration for ['Revolution'] was the May '68 student uprising in Paris, which reached its crescendo with de Gaulle's dissolution of the French National Assembly on the very evening [May 30] that 'Revolution #1' was being laid down in London," wrote Beatles chronicler Ian MacDonald in his book *Revolution in the Head: The Beatles Records and the Sixties.*

But rather than support the revolution, "Revolution" advised protestors to change themselves first. The lines "If you go around carrying pictures of Chairman Mao/You ain't gonna make it with anyone anyhow" and "Don't you know it's gonna be alright" were seen as a sell-out by those who sought to overturn the political structure of the West. "The New Left and countercultural press were... offended, especially in America," wrote MacDonald, "where 'Revolution' was branded a 'betrayal' and 'a lamentable petty bourgeois cry of fear.'"

Lennon, though, may have been ahead of the curve. Radicals may have objected, and the Doors might have sung: "They've got the guns but we've got the numbers," but in 1968, to paraphrase a well-known aphorism of Chairman Mao's, power came from the barrel of a gun.

JUNE: "IS THERE A DOCTOR IN THE HOUSE?"

○─◉─○

here was no honor in the manner in which Robert F. Kennedy entered the 1968 presidential race. His closest advisers had, after all, strongly suggested to him that he'd be better off waiting for 1972, when Lyndon Johnson's all but inevitable final term would be finished—and Kennedy seemed inclined to take their advice.

But then Eugene McCarthy showed in the New Hampshire primary that LBJ was vulnerable.

Time magazine would later, in a 1998 essay on 1968, call Kennedy's entrance "sheepish and vaguely ignominious, piggybacking on Eugene McCarthy's courage."

But Kennedy came to show his own courage. As Washington, D.C., burned in the wake of the King assassination, Robert Kennedy walked the streets of the ghetto inferno, perhaps the only white face without a gun and badge. He was greeted with awe and appreciation.

"Is that you?" a black woman asked, not believing her eyes. "I knew you'd be the first to come here, darling."

Despite ambivalence toward Kennedy's entry, McCarthy's erratic, directionless campaigning was no match for the Kennedy charisma. Bobby Kennedy won important primaries in Indiana and

Nebraska. But in unpredictable, independent-minded Oregon, McCarthy snatched back the momentum with an upset win. No one could remember a Kennedy ever losing an election before, anywhere.

All eyes were on June 4's California primary. For Kennedy, California had everything that Oregon did not: numerous large media markets and substantial numbers of poor citizens of color who seemed to feed off Kennedy's emotionalism—and vice versa. Kennedy won in the Golden State, though not by the large margin pundits had predicted. Yet the large crowd in Los Angeles's Ambassador Hotel shared Kennedy's jubilation. "My thanks to you all," he told his supporters that night, "and on to Chicago, and let's win there." He then headed off through the hotel kitchen toward the press room. Writer Jules Witcover was there.

"As Kennedy turned to look for his wife, the

BOBBY KENNEDY'S
ASSASSINATION
LEFT MANY PEOPLE
FRIGHTENED,
DISCOURAGED,
AND COMPLETELY
DISILLUSIONED.

young man standing on the tray stacker stepped down, raised his right hand high over the crowd, and fired a snub-nosed revolver at Kennedy's head from only a few feet away. ...I turned and saw Kennedy already fallen on his back, his eyes open, arms over his bleeding head, his feet apart."

Two of Kennedy's aides, former Olympic champion Rafer Johnson and professional football player Rosie Greer, grabbed the gunman's arm. Andrew West, a reporter for the Mutual Radio Network, had been standing next to Kennedy, his tape recorder running, when the shots that felled the candidate were fired from a .22 caliber pistol:

"I am right here and Rafer Johnson has hold of the man who apparently has fired the shot! He has fired the shot. ...He still has the gun! The gun is pointed right at me at this moment! I hope they can get the gun out of his hand. Be very careful. Get the gun...get the gun...stay away from the gun.

...Get his thumb, get his thumb, get his thumb. ...Get away from the barrel! Get away from the barrel, man! Look out for the gun!...Okay, all right. That's it, Rafer, get it! Get the gun, Rafer! Okay, now hold on to the gun. ...Ladies and gentlemen, they have the gun away from the man...."

A young campaign worker stood at the podium where Kennedy had spoken only moments before and, speaking into the microphone, asked the crowd, "Is there a doctor in the house?"

But it was too late. Despite hours of surgery, Kennedy never recovered consciousness and was pronounced dead after midnight, June 6.

His killer was identified as Sirhan Sirhan, a Jordanian born in Jerusalem who had lived in Los Angeles since 1957. Sirhan's apparent motive: Kennedy's support for Israel. Notes were found among Sirhan's belongings that "Robert F. Kennedy must be assassinated before 5 June 1968." June 5

"SOME MEN
SEE THINGS AS THEY ARE AND SAY
WHY.
I DREAM THINGS
THAT NEVER WERE
AND SAY
WHY NOT."

was the first anniversary of Israel's devastating defeat of its Arab enemies in the Six Day War of 1967.

The country was consumed by almost inconsolable grief. A former rockabilly singer named Dick Holler wrote a song—sung by Dion, another seemingly out-of-place fifties rocker—that would resound with the sadness so universally felt by the murders of Bobby Kennedy and three other American leaders: "Abraham, Martin and John."

The assassinated triumvirate recalled in the title—Abraham Lincoln, Martin Luther King, and John F. Kennedy—was joined in a final verse by Bobby Kennedy.

The press corps, too, took the second Kennedy assassination as more of a personal loss than might have been expected. But like his brother, Robert Kennedy enjoyed close relationships with many reporters. Jules Witcover was one such insider.

"In part it was a result of age and shared generational outlook," he wrote of Kennedy after his death. "In part it stemmed from respect for the man he was becoming more than the man he had been in his brusquer days. We had seen at close range his evolution from a rude, arrogant brat...to a wrenchingly troubled heir to a political legacy that had increasingly taken him out of himself and made him a public man, espousing the public good."

Kennedy's body was flown to New York, where his closed casket was to be viewed by the public at St. Patrick's Cathedral the next morning. People lined the streets over night. The viewing was to end at 10 P.M. But the huge throngs continued lining up for a last look throughout the day and into the night.

A slow train carried Kennedy from New York's Penn Station to burial in Arlington National Cemetery. Mourners stood by to pay their respects at each station and along the tracks. (Near Elizabeth, New Jersey, a family of mourners was killed by a northbound train; after that, train traffic was suspended in both directions for the Kennedy cortege). The next day, in Washington's brutal summertime heat and humidity, an estimated 50,000 mourners visited RFK's grave.

At RFK's funeral at St. Patrick's Cathedral, Edward M. Kennedy, who had seen three older brothers die, two to assassins' bullets, gave what many thought the most eloquent address of his long and distinguished life:

"My brother need not be idealized, or enlarged in death beyond what he was in life, to be remembered simply as a good and decent man, who saw wrong and tried to right it, saw suffering and tried to heal it, saw war and tried to stop it.

"Those of us who loved him and who take him to his rest today, pray that what he was to us and what he wished for others will some day come to pass for all the world.

"As he said many times, in many parts of this nation, to those he touched and who sought to touch him:

'Some men see things as they are and say why.
I dream things that never were and say why not.'"

In a year of shocking images, that of the mortally wounded Kennedy may have been the most profoundly shattering. "The sudden sense of vacancy, of eternity, in Robert Kennedy's eyes as he lay on the floor of the Los Angeles hotel pantry. That vacancy, almost exactly halfway through the year, seemed to break the year's back. Nothing good, one thought, could happen after that," wrote *Time*'s Lance Morrow, years afterward.

Bobby Kennedy's assassination left many frightened, discouraged, and completely disillusioned. As P. J. O'Rourke remembers, "It seemed like America was turning into this horrible monster that...was eating a lot of people at that time." There was an increasing sense, as O'Rourke puts it, "that the country really might start to be ripped apart."

The Rolling Stones, working in the studio on their album *Beggars Banquet,* rewrote "Sympathy for the Devil" the day after the assassination to include the line "I shouted out, 'Who killed the Kennedys?'" As Tim White puts it, "The Stones really saw their music in a lot of ways as...the headlines."

In America, David Crosby, of Crosby, Stills & Nash, saw the killing as "ballot by bullet...no good." Young people who were trying to get involved in politics and, as Crosby sees it, "a lot of the dropout from participating in the country as a whole... happened because here we had guys that we'd believed in, three of them in a row shot down. ...It started to bring us right out of it."

Crosby's personal reaction to the killing manifested itself in his song "Long Time Gone," which he wrote the day after. "I liked Bobby," he says today, "I thought he was a good guy, tough guy, good sense of reality and a good set of ethics."

Crosby tried to get Big Brother and the Holding Company to record the song, as band member Dave Getz remembers, coming to the CBS studio where Big Brother was recording and playing the song for them on electric guitar. "This is a great response," thought Getz at the time, but it was ultimately Crosby, Stills & Nash who recorded the heartfelt tribute to America's slain heroes.

On the afternoon of Robert Kennedy's funeral, there was another news bulletin. Police in London had arrested suspected King assassin James Earl Ray with a loaded gun at Heathrow Airport.

Ray had escaped North America on a forged Canadian passport. Two members of the Royal Canadian Mounted Police had gone through 200,000 passport application photos. The Mounties got their man. But was he the right man? Or the only man?

For a common convict like Ray to have escaped the biggest manhunt in American history for two hours, much less two months, strained credibility. The fact that showing up at Heathrow,

THE KING AND KENNEDY ASSASSINATIONS BROUGHT THE NATIONAL PSYCHE CLOSE TO A BREAKDOWN AS LOGIC AND PARANOIA WRESTLED TO A STANDOFF.

the most security-conscious airport in the free world, with a loaded gun, made many think that Ray hardly had the intelligence, the savvy, or the resources to be the lone assassin. In fact, Ray, a barely literate redneck, couldn't even convincingly explain what he was doing in England.

Ray pled guilty to shooting King and was sentenced to ninety-nine years in prison. But on March 10, 1969, he would tell the court that, while he disagreed with the prosecution theory that there had been no conspiracy he would not provide any information in support of this. Judge W. Preston Battle issued a carefully worded statement that the fact that the prosecution did not have sufficient evidence to indict any co-conspirators was, "of course, not conclusive evidence that there was no conspiracy."

Such muted denials did not reassure those who thought King, like John F. Kennedy, may not have been the victim of an isolated individual killer. And even until Ray's death in prison from liver disease a few years ago, the survivors of Martin Luther King Jr., including his widow, Coretta, and his children, believed that Ray was telling the truth—that he was not the lone gunman.

The King and Kennedy assassinations brought the national psyche close to a breakdown as logic and paranoia wrestled to a standoff. In his novel *1968*, based on the events of the year, Joe Haldeman wrote: "Maybe our desire to see these assassinations as the work of large mysterious forces beyond our control is a way of denying the simple truth: in America, any nutcase with the price of a gun obviously has a fair prospect of killing any public figure he dislikes."

1968

CHAPTER FIVE

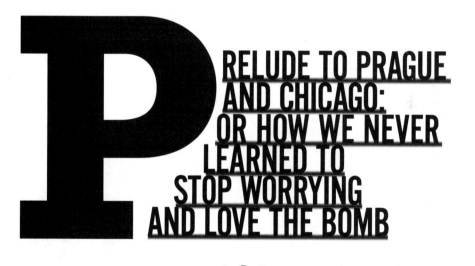

RELUDE TO PRAGUE
AND CHICAGO:
OR HOW WE NEVER
LEARNED TO
STOP WORRYING
AND LOVE THE BOMB

 he 1950s, during which the youth generation of 1968
grew up, were considered prosperous and relatively safe
years. But an undercurrent of anxiety rippled through the decade.

The fear was of nothing less than the world being destroyed by atomic war. Distant as that notion seems now in the post–Cold War world when the United States is for the moment the world's sole superpower, that fear was a visceral and sometimes visible presence in American life.

"The world really began for us," Abbie Hoffman once said, "on August 6, 1945, when the atomic bomb was dropped."

Schoolchildren as early as kindergarten were subjected to air raid drills. When the sirens blew, we were trained to calmly line up, go into the hallway, and kneel down with our heads facing the wall. We were trained that if the attack was sudden and immediate, to hide under our desks and avert our faces from the windows so as not to be hurt by flying glass during our annihilation at the hands of Russian or Chinese bombs.

"Our generation was really open to taking chances," said Jefferson Airplane's Paul Kantner. "It might have been coming from years of being told to hide under our desk when they drop the atomic bomb, and that will protect us [laughs] when they drop a five-hundred-kiloton atomic device…"

The most paranoid of that generation's parents—and there were many—built underground bomb shelters in the backyard filled with canned foods and bottled water. In this way would well-prepared Americans survive an atomic attack, to emerge when the radiation dissipated.

The fear permeated the popular culture as well. Movie theaters were filled with films dealing literally and metaphorically with nuclear war or totalitarian conquest.

They ranged from witty parables like *Invasion of the Body Snatchers* to edgy survivalist dramas like *Panic in Year Zero* to monster movies such as *Godzilla*, *The Thing*, and *It Came From Outer Space*.

By the early 1960s more realistic nuclear dramas such as *Fail Safe* and *Seven Days in May* were showing how mechanical and human failure could override supposedly infallible precautionary measures and ignite nuclear war.

The genius of Stanley Kubrick's 1964 movie *Dr. Strangelove: or How I Learned to Stop Worrying and Love the Bomb* was that it exposed those subterranean fears, hilariously reveling in the insanity of an arms race the military seemed helpless, or unwilling, to stop.

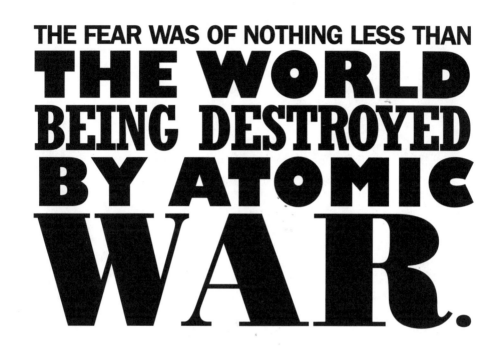

THE FEAR WAS OF NOTHING LESS THAN THE WORLD BEING DESTROYED BY ATOMIC WAR.

MORE THAN 55,000 AMERICANS

AND PERHAPS HUNDREDS OF THOUSANDS OF

VIETNAMESE WOULD DIE

FOR NO APPARENT REASON

BECAUSE THE PRESIDENTS AND GENERALS IN CHARGE

COULD NOT FIGURE OUT

A WAY TO LEAVE VIETNAM

WITHOUT LOSING FACE.

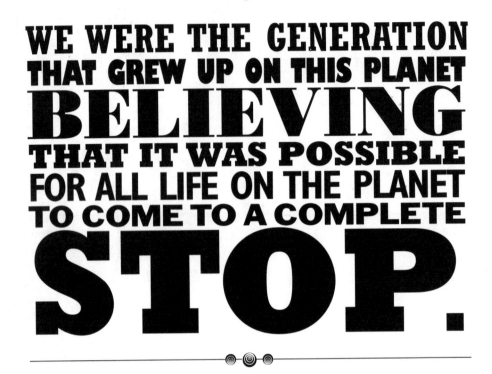

WE WERE THE GENERATION THAT GREW UP ON THIS PLANET BELIEVING THAT IT WAS POSSIBLE FOR ALL LIFE ON THE PLANET TO COME TO A COMPLETE STOP.

"Conceptually, we had already been living with the bomb," Pauline Kael wrote in a famous 1967 essay. "Now the mass audience of the movies—which is the youth of America—grasped the idea that the threat of extinction can be used to devaluate everything, to turn it all into a joke."

The name given to the rise of apocalyptic comedy in the 1960s was "black humor." Shining examples included novels like Joseph Heller's *Catch-22*, Kurt Vonnegut's *Mother Night* and *Slaughterhouse-Five*, and Thomas Pynchon's *The Crying of Lot 49*.

All were set in World War II, yet each had a message clear to the youth of the 1960s. Influential literary and social critic Morris Dickstein saw these books as anticipating the "moral nausea of the Vietnam War."

In 1968, the Cold War was intact—but so was a ground and air war in an Asian country halfway around the world with which America had no conventional or convincing ties; where more than 55,000 Americans and perhaps hundreds of thousands of Vietnamese would die for no apparent reason because the presidents and generals in charge could not figure out a way to leave Vietnam without losing face. Mix this with the assassinations of Martin Luther King and Robert F. Kennedy, and you have a generation raised in physical comfort but emotionally on edge ready to believe that the sky might have been falling.

"When we lost Bobby Kennedy and Martin Luther King there's the natural feeling of, 'How freaky is this American scene? How far will it go?'" Art Garfunkel said. "When you have the rug pulled out from under you, you then say, 'Will the earth be pulled out from under?' You know, we lived in those days with the fear of nuclear war. We knew that the earth could be pulled out from under us. There

could be a nuclear catastrophe falling on any American city."

Songs like "Wooden Ships," written by David Crosby and Paul Kantner and performed by both Crosby, Stills & Nash and Jefferson Airplane, exposed this fear. "We were the generation that grew up believing that it was possible for all life on the planet to come to a complete stop," Crosby says. "We're the only generation that ever grew up that way. The only ones that had a full stop in our lexicon. An end. ...Back then we lived in fear of a nuclear holocaust that would end life on the planet, or at least severely reduce the number of people." "Wooden Ships" is, as Crosby puts it, "the great postapocalyptic fantasy."

Such fear, however, helped unite the young generation throughout the world. It was a generation defined as "post-Hiroshima," a group that British writer and musician Jeff Nuttall defined as

Bomb Culture in the title of his influential 1968 book. Nuttall offers a British view of the phenomenon of 1968.

"What has happened is that the pressure of restriction preceding nuclear suicide has precipitated a biological reflex compelling the leftist element in the young middle class to join with the delinquent element in the young working class for the reaffirmation of life by orgy and violence..."

In marches, demonstrations, strikes, riots, and in their cultural expression, long defined by the trilogy of sex, drugs, and rock and roll, the established order rules were under assault by those driven to nausea by fear of the bomb. "Young people are not correcting society. They are regurgitating it." This barf reflex was set off in Europe during the last week or so of August 1968, by the events in Czechoslovakia, and in the United States during the Democratic National Convention.

CHAPTER SIX

THE PRAGUE SPRING

The uprisings in 1968 against the established order in so many places involved students or young people acting against adult authority. Not so in Czechoslovakia, where the season of openness and change that became known as the Prague Spring started at the top: With Alexander Dubček, top man in the Czechoslovakian Communist Party.

Dubček had been a loyal member of the party for thirty years. But like many moderates, he was troubled by the murderous, repressive rule of Soviet dictator Josef Stalin. When Dubček took office as first secretary of the party (essentially, the prime minister) in January 1968, he was able to enact the reforms that he called "Socialism with a human face."

Censorship was gone. The state-owned newspapers, radio, and television stations were allowed to print and broadcast freely. Writers, artists, and musicians, who had been repressed, even beaten and imprisoned for their work under the formerly rigid Communist regime, were free to express themselves.

Miroslav Galuska, a Czech journalist who had been exiled by the previous leaders, returned to find himself named cultural minister.

"I wanted to liberalize culture from the dictation of power and the dictation of money," recalled Galuska in a 1999 Central Europe Online special feature. "We abolished censorship of the press and censorship of the arts. We had no time

to decide what would happen. Suddenly you had newspaper people who had been controlled for so long not having any bosses. ...There was total freedom bordering on anarchy. We went too far too fast."

Too far, too fast. Too much, too soon. That was certainly the conclusion of the grim hardliners who found themselves a minority in the Czech Communist Party. Fear of freedom spread to the leadership of nearby Eastern Bloc countries such as East Germany and Poland. The Czech party's apparent loss of control was also viewed with alarm in the Soviet Union, which would not allow its Warsaw Pact allies to simply wander away.

Despite warnings from Moscow, Dubček would not squeeze the genie back into the lamp. On August 21—one week before the Chicago Democratic Convention—200,000 Russian troops entered Czechoslovakia, a country roughly the size of Ohio, to end the threat of freedom.

The first dramatic word of the invasion came from Radio Prague. "Friends, I think these will soon

"FRIENDS, I THINK THESE WILL SOON BE **THE LAST WORDS** YOU WILL HEAR FROM US. FRIENDS, WE ALL BELIEVE, **I ASK YOU, URGENTLY,** BELIEVE THAT HEALTHY THINKING **MUST WIN.** YOU HEAR THE **SHOOTING."**

be the last words you will hear from us. Friends, we all believe, I ask you urgently, believe that healthy thinking must win. You hear the shooting."

Whoever controlled the mass media controlled the country, so it was not surprising that the Russian tanks would make their first stop at Radio Prague. Twenty people were killed in the battle for the station. But ironically, aware of the importance of the radio, the Russians had years before helped Czechoslovakia build an alternative, underground radio network, in case of invasion by the West.

For a full week, the underground radio brought the country a message that urged nonviolent resistance to the Soviets. In a brilliant stroke, citizens were asked to remove all street and highway signs to confuse their unwelcome visitors. Within days, the only signs visible to the Russian army were those pointing to Moscow.

Dubček was arrested and brought to Moscow, where he was tortured into signing a paper acknowledging the legitimacy of Russia's military presence in Czechoslovakia. He was then returned to Prague, where he briefly held power again in name only.

Soon stripped of his title as well as his office, Dubček was exiled to the countryside, where he was given a job fixing chain saws.

Dubček's replacement was Gustáv Husák, a hard-liner who for the next twenty years set Czechoslovakia back to total Communist repression.

Particularly hard hit were the artists, musicians, and writers who had briefly blossomed in what became known as the Prague Spring. A rock band called the Plastic People of the Universe formed immediately after the Russian Invasion, named after a Frank Zappa song that appeared on the Mothers of Invention's 1967 album, *Absolutely Free.*

Zappa was beloved in Czechoslovakia and his music had been smuggled into the country since the mid-'60s. When Zappa visited Prague, he learned that he was considered one of the worst enemies of the Communist state. As one journalist recounts the story, one student told of being

ZAPPA USED A BROAD MUSICAL PALETTE TO LAMPOON EVERYTHING FROM THE VIETNAM WAR TO TV COMMERCIALS TO THE WEEKEND HIPPIES AND PART-TIME POTHEADS WHO WERE TURNING THE COUNTERCULTURE INTO A TIE-DYED THEME PARK.

arrested by the secret police and beaten. "'We are going to beat the Frank Zappa music out of your head,' the officer screamed."

Zappa, rock's premiere satirist, and his versatile, virtuoso group, the Mothers of Invention, used a broad musical palette to lampoon everything from the Vietnam War to TV commercials to the weekend hippies and part-time potheads who were turning the counterculture into a tie-dyed theme park.

Zappa, who died of prostate cancer in 1993, was also a most lucid and fearless proponent of free speech and free thought. And the seeds that were planted before and during 1968 in Czechoslovakia ultimately bloomed twenty-one years later. In 1989, as Communist regimes toppled, the writer and playwright Vaclev Havel, a devoted fan of Zappa, found himself the free country's president.

Havel had spent the early summer of 1968 in New York, where one of his plays was being performed at Joseph Papp's New York Shakespeare Festival. Havel visited the Columbia strikers in May and hung around the East Village. (As writer Paul Berman notes, Zappa and the Mothers of Invention were playing the Fillmore East in the same neighborhood.) An intellectual and rock and roll fan, Havel returned to Czechoslovakia clutching a Velvet Underground album.

The Velvets and Zappa were the direct inspiration for the music of the often-jailed Plastic People of the Universe, keeping the spirit of rock and freedom alive during Czechoslovakia's dark decades after 1968. When Havel was named president in 1989, one of his first acts was to invite Zappa to a state visit.

Havel named Zappa a special ambassador to the West on trade, tourism, and culture. But President Reagan's Secretary of State, James Baker, forced Havel to withdraw the offer. A few years later, however, when Havel made a state visit to President Clinton, he asked that Lou Reed perform. Havel told Reed that the Velvets had changed Czech history.

Christ died
for Yippie! CHICAGO
AUG. 25-30
Rom. 5-6

CHICAGO SUMMER

espite the worst fears of the straight world, Abbie Hoffman and Jerry Rubin were not Communists inspired by Karl Marx and V. I. Lenin: They were, rather, antic media manipulators inspired by Groucho Marx and John Lennon. In 1967, while many other long hairs were luxuriating in peace and love as hippies, Hoffman and Rubin founded an organization called the Youth International Party: Yippies, for short.

Yippie was born, appropriately, at a New Year's Eve get-together with Abbie Hoffman and Paul Krassner, editor of the satirical antiestablishment magazine *The Realist*. Rubin describes the birth of the yippies in his stream-of-consciousness book, *Do It!*

> We got very stoned so we could look at
> at the problem logically:
> It's a youth revolution
> Gimme a "Y."
> It's an international revolution.
> Gimme an "I."
> It's people trying to have meaning, fun,
> ecstasy in their lives—a party.
> Gimme a "P."
> Youth International Party.
> Paul Krassner jumped to his feet and
> shouted: "YIP-pie! We're yippies!"
> A movement was born.

The "movement" was mostly in Rubin, Hoffman, and Krassner's minds: Rubin called it a "nonorganization," but it made for delicious propaganda. And in a nonsensical way, it filled a void, to describe a new breed of youth who were too apolitical for SDS, too ornery for Flower Power, too irreverent to be intellectual.

"A stoned politico. A hybrid mixture of New Left and hippie," is how Rubin described the party. But then, always, came the rush of hyperbole. The yippie was "a streetfighting freek [sic], a dropout, who carries a gun at his hip. So ugly that middle-class society is frightened by how he looks. A long-haired, bearded, hairy, crazy motherfucker whose life is theater, every moment creating the new society as he destroys the old."

Such a person didn't really exist, but that was no problem. The yippies were masters at the comedic guerrilla warfare known as street theater. During a major 1967 antiwar demonstration in Washington, D.C., Hoffman and Rubin had led thousands in a mock attempt to "levitate" the Pentagon building. Later that year they caused a revealing melee at the New York Stock Exchange when they threw dollar bills onto the trading floor from the Visitor's Gallery.

The "Festival of Life" Hoffman and Rubin planned as a counterpoint to the August 1968 Democratic National Convention in Chicago was to be their coup de grace. "Yippies would use the Democratic Party and the Chicago theater to build our stage and make the myth," Rubin later wrote. "We'd steal the media away from the Democrats and create the specter of 'yippies' overthrowing Amerika."

"WE GOT VERY STONED SO WE COULD LOOK AT THE PROBLEM LOGICALLY: **IT'S A YOUTH REVOLUTION. GIMME A 'Y'.** ITS AN INTERNATIONAL REVOLUTION. **GIMME AN 'I'.** IT'S PEOPLE TRYING TO HAVE **MEANING, FUN, ECSTACY IN THEIR LIVES—A PARTY. GIMME A 'P'.** YOUTH INTERNATIONAL PARTY."

Circumstances played into yippie plans. Liberal hopes that an antiwar candidate would wrest the nomination away from the party establishment had collapsed in the wake of Bobby Kennedy's assassination. Dismayed and possibly afraid for his own life amid the year's violence, Eugene McCarthy's campaign style had deteriorated from indifference to something approaching disorientation.

Norman Mailer, in his groundbreaking book about the 1968 political conventions, *Miami and the Siege of Chicago*, described running into McCarthy at a cocktail party a week after Kennedy's assassination: "He looked weary beyond belief, his skin a used-up yellow, his tall body serving for no more than to keep his head up above the crowd at the cocktail party."

Though Mailer was fond of McCarthy he had been a bigger fan of Robert Kennedy, and he could see that the poetry-writing Minnesota senator didn't have the fire in his belly to make a hard run at the presidency, much less be president.

"He seemed," said Mailer, "more like the dean of the finest English department in the land."

Vice President Hubert H. Humphrey, marshaling the commanding logistical advantage of the mainstream Democratic Party, arrived in Chicago in August with the nomination all but guaranteed.

The host of the convention was Democratic Mayor Richard Daley, the very picture of the horse-trading, backroom autocrat, a big-city power broker. It has long been suggested, and never disproven, that John F. Kennedy's razor-thin victory over Nixon in the 1960 presidential election could be credited to Daley, who was gifted at turning out the vote of even the dead.

Chicago wasn't Daley's city, it was his fiefdom. When Chicago's black neighborhoods exploded after the Martin Luther King assassination, Daley had given orders to his police and the National Guard to shoot to kill if they came upon looters.

Daley was the face of the Democratic mainstream, and he'd rigged the convention in the crammed Chicago Amphitheatre for Humphrey's nomination. Appalled by yippie rhetoric that they'd

dose the city's water supply with LSD and send hippie chicks to seduce convention delegates, Daley refused to grant the demonstrators a permit to march, demonstrate, or hold a concert. Daley, in fact, arranged for a paramilitary display by the Chicago police both inside and outside the convention hall.

It's an indication of how sour things had gone so quickly in the counterculture that none of the famous rock groups the yippies invited to perform in Chicago decided to make the trip.

"I didn't want to go there," said Dave Getz, drummer for Big Brother and the Holding Company, Janis Joplin's breakthrough band. "By that time, the whole yippie thing, I thought, was fraught with confrontation and danger. ...We took the point of view that these guys [Hoffman and Rubin] are like kind of clowns."

The Jefferson Airplane, whose songs had become anthems of opposition to the status quo, remained grounded as well.

"The results of the Democratic convention were going to be very obvious and old by the time [they] came out," Paul Kantner said. "From going up against the police at the Fillmore Auditorium when we wanted to open it up with Bill Graham and work there and do it our way, we had gone though those protests and that kind of action. ...It needed doing and I applaud them for doing it, but we had already done that, and it was apparent that you were going up against a force that was not going to respond to you appropriately."

David Crosby of Crosby, Stills & Nash echoes this sentiment. He didn't want to have anything to do with playing in Chicago because he thought protesting the Convention was beside the point. As he puts it, "At that time I wouldn't have participated in politics for all the tea in China. I was fully outside the system."

As it was, from the protest-oriented folksinger community only Phil Ochs showed up in Chicago. And MC5 was the only big rock band there. MC5 stood for Motor City Five. Detroit, with its legacy of

union activism and power, was one of the few places in America where blue-collar youth lined up on the side of stoned activism.

"It was kind of standard operating procedure for the MC5 to play at political events, rallies, or

antiwar protests," Wayne Kramer, one of the band's guitarists, said. "We heard there was going to be a Festival of Life in Chicago. Jerry Rubin and Abbie Hoffman were good friends with John Sinclair, our manager, and so they said, 'we're going to have an alternative to the Democratic Convention'—[which] we viewed as the Festival of Death.

"We knew it was probably going to be creepy as far as the Chicago Police Department went. We were pretty battle-hardened veterans ourselves. We had been in a bunch of riot situations with the Detroit Police Department, with the Oakland County Sheriff...so we kind of knew what to expect. This wasn't a big secret that these forces were going to meet here and there, there was going to be a clash."

Kramer also recalls that the Grateful Dead, Jefferson Airplane, and Big Brother and the Holding

THE SENSE OF MENACE WAS VERY REAL.
NOT JUST FROM THE MASSIVE
POLICE PRESENCE
VISIBLE AROUND THE PARK
BUT FROM A LARGE CONTINGENT OF
UNDERCOVER POLICE,
MILITARY INTELLIGENCE OFFICERS,
AND PAID PROVOCATEURS
AMID THE DEMONSTRATORS.
IT MAY SOUND LIKE
PARANOIA
IN THIS DAY AND AGE, BUT BY MOST ACCOUNTS
IT WAS TRUE.

Company were supposed to be coming to Chicago. Whether it was ever true or just yippie hype from the beginning hardly matters.

But Kramer understood where these other bands were coming from—or, not coming from. "I think, in all fairness, they were afraid of the Chicago Police Department. They were afraid of what was going to happen. For the MC5, you know, it was kind of normal for us. We were young, and we were ambitious, and we were committed, and you know, we were arrogant. We were crazy and we were right."

The tension in Lincoln Park was palpable on Sunday, August 25, the day before the convention was to begin. Leaflets and placards urging people to "Vote Pig in 68" dotted the crowd—the yippies were nominating an actual sow named Pigasus for president.

Because they lacked a permit, police wouldn't let the MC5's stage and power supply—a flatbed truck with a generator—through the crowd. So the MC5 just plugged their equipment into a hot dog stand outlet and played on the level ground. Their trademark shout of "Kick out the jams, motherfuckers!" soon rose up from the crowd.

The sense of menace was very real. Not just from the massive police presence visible around the park but from a large contingent of undercover police, military intelligence officers, and paid provocateurs amid the demonstrators. It may sound like paranoia in this day and age, but by most accounts it was true.

Norman Mailer, covering the conventions for *Harper's* magazine, caught "the bird of fear beginning to nest in the throat" as he took notes in Chicago that afternoon. "The air of Lincoln Park came into the nose with that tender concern which air seemed always ready to offer when danger announced its presence."

"It wasn't like a rock concert, there wasn't any joy in the air," Kramer recalls. "There were these guys in Army fatigue jackets with short hair and aviator sunglasses...going around starting fights

with people, and the Chicago Police Department were riding their motorcycles through the middle of the crowd, knocking people over. It was tense. Because you know the shit was going to hit the fan at some point. And I knew when that point would be because," he says, laughing, "I had played at a lot of riots before." It was the point when "the band stops playing, and all this energy starts to...search around.

"We played, and did our set, and we rocked. And the people were into it, we were doing this free music section, because a lot of the MC5's work was informed by the work of Sun Ra and John Coltrane...in this rock music we were performing. ...And all of a sudden it was like the Army helicopters were coming down on top of the band with these *whump-whump-whump-whump* sounds." When they stopped playing, sure enough, the riot began. The Chicago Police charged through the crowd, beating people left and right. What Kramer saw was "just a rampage...like a cavalry charge, or like those kinds of films about medieval warriors?

You know, the whole group comes charging down the hill, kind of like a *Braveheart* thing?" As it turned out, though, Sunday in the park with the MC5 had merely whet the Chicago Police's appetite for destruction.

The next day the Democratic Convention began on a high note with Aretha Franklin singing the National Anthem inside the Chicago Amphitheatre. It was the convention's first, last, and only moment of truth, beauty, and soul. As CBS anchorman Walter Cronkite told his tens of millions of viewers: "The convention belongs in a Police State. No other way to put it."

When Dan Rather, then an aggressive, young reporter on the convention floor, told Cronkite, at his anchor desk, that Mayor Daley had banned any demonstrations inside the hall, he was punched in the stomach by one of Daley's men. "I think we've got a bunch of thugs here, Dan," a fuming Cronkite said on the air. Shortly thereafter, another star CBS reporter, Mike Wallace, was punched out by a policeman before being arrested.

At the same time that Soviet tanks were rolling into Czechoslovakia to crush the Prague Spring, Chicago was home to its own show of oppression. In Grant Park, demonstrators, shouting, "the whole world is watching!" tried to put the American flag there at half-mast.

Again the cops went berserk, beating and clubbing the crowd indiscriminately. Not just demonstrators but reporters and innocent bystanders—pregnant women, senior citizens, whoever got in their way. As one who was there described, it was "a free-for-all on worldwide television with young people and others just getting bloodied senseless."

P. J. O'Rourke sees the events in Chicago as expressions of some of the same fault lines of class that had opened over the war in Vietnam. It was, as he puts it flatly, "Class warfare—but not the kind that we thought...we thought we were upholding the impoverished and the downtrodden in America. In fact, the impoverished and the downtrodden had gotten jobs at the police department and were busting us over the head."

It was, literally, a police riot. And it chastened and infuriated many of the Democratic party leaders. When Senator Abraham Ribicoff of Connecticut placed the name of George McGovern in nomination he stared at Mayor Daley and said the party should not tolerate "Gestapo tactics on the streets of Chicago."

A national television audience heard Ribicoff's words and saw Daley's emphatic response. Flipping Ribicoff the finger, Daley's lips seemed to be saying, "Get out of here, you Hebe," or some variation of "dirty Jew."

There was, in the words of antiwar protestor Ronnie Davis, "a sense that the brutality of Vietnam was now coming home."

Hubert H. Humphrey won the nomination, but party unity was broken beyond repair. "The Happy Warrior," as he had been called as a youthful liberal

AGAIN THE COPS WENT BERSERK, **BEATING AND CLUBBING** THE CROWD INDISCRIMINATELY. NOT JUST DEMONSTRATORS, **BUT REPORTERS** AND INNOCENT BYSTANDERS— **PREGNANT WOMEN,** SENIOR CITIZENS, WHOEVER GOT IN THEIR WAY.

firebrand, would not or could not completely disavow Lyndon Johnson's Vietnam policy. The third party candidacy of Alabama Governor George Wallace, a champion of segregation, siphoned votes from the once rock-solid traditional Southern Democratic base.

Richard Nixon, meanwhile, had chosen Maryland Governor Spiro T. Agnew as his vice presidential running mate. Agnew had once been a pillar of the Republican party's moderate wing: He had, in fact, strongly supported the candidacy of the party's last liberal, Nelson Rockefeller.

But Agnew had shown Nixon his mettle in castigating the Maryland black leaders (who had supported him) for not doing more to keep order in their community when Baltimore joined the roster of American cities torn by riots after the King assassination. Agnew became Nixon's attack dog in a campaign that had them hammering away at Democrats, blacks, students, and the antiwar movement as unpatriotic swing. Their "law and order" campaign was crafted to build on the fears of what Nixon had dubbed "the Silent Majority." The chaos of Chicago certainly played into Nixon's hands, even though it had been the police who had rioted.

For American liberals, Chicago was part of, as P. J. O'Rourke puts it, "a long string of disillusionment...starting with the assassination of JFK, then the expansion of the war in Vietnam and intensifying with the year's two other assassinations ('especially King')."

The year was breaking America's back and spirit, and the summer wasn't even over yet.

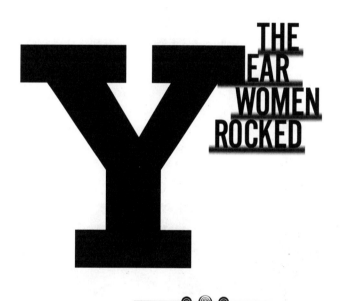

THE YEAR WOMEN ROCKED

he country may have been falling apart but rock and roll was flourishing. In 1968 it was enjoying a period of great artistry and innovation. And one popular music trend in particular reflected the tenor of the times—while women in society at large pushed for equal rights, 1968 was a year in which strong female artists came to dominate the charts as well.

The emergence of compelling new female singers like Jefferson Airplane's Grace Slick and Big Brother and the Holding Company's Janis Joplin, along with landmark hits and career moves by established artists like Aretha Franklin and Diana Ross (who became a truly solo act in 1968), made it a banner year for women who did not fit the traditional mold of the "chick singer." Diva, perhaps; chick singer, no.

And as historian Charles Kaiser put it, "Grace Slick and Janis Joplin and Aretha Franklin [were] really contributing to the feminist movement indirectly because they [were] just as famous and just as important as any male rock and roll star, so you see real artistic equality between men and women."

Grace Slick had joined the already established Jefferson Airplane in 1966. The following year, her vocal on the hit "Somebody to Love," off of the sublimely strange *After Bathing at Baxter's*, introduced the world to what would become one of rock's most recognizable voices—a regal, even haughty alto or mezzo soprano singing at the very upper limit of her rage and combining a freaked-out psychedelic abandon with utter, cool control. In 1967, Slick gave heads their marching orders—"Go ask Alice..."—in the hit "White Rabbit."

Slick turned in a bravura vocal performance on "White Rabbit," in many ways her signature song—at turns commanding and vulnerable, dreamy and unyielding. It, and her unusual, direct good looks, made her a pop icon—the Rock and Roll Ice Queen. Or, as bandmate Paul Kantner puts it, "Grace was a fuck-off model who could sing real good."

In 1968 Jefferson Airplane was at the height of its success and Slick was continuing in her role as the finger-pointing siren of rock and roll. The Airplane was at the time a band with a fair amount of political commentary and content in their songs, and on recordings such as that year's "Crown of Creation" (from the album of the same name), Slick's keening, cutting-cold vocals gave the songs a visceral authority that went beyond their lyrics.

In a time of rapidly evolving sexual and gender mores, women like Slick were in many ways

IN A TIME OF RAPIDLY EVOLVING SEXUAL AND GENDER MORES, **WOMEN LIKE SLICK** WERE IN MANY WAYS AT THE **VANGUARD**, IF AT TIMES UNWITTINGLY SO. CERTAINLY SLICK MORE THAN ONCE **FOUND HERSELF FAR AHEAD** OF EVEN THE EXPECTATIONS A **ROCK AND ROLL CROWD** MIGHT HAVE FOR A **FEMALE LEAD SINGER.**

IF FEMALE SINGERS LIKE GRACE SLICK BROKE THE MOLD OF THE "CHICK" OR GIRL SINGER, JANIS JOPLIN SEEMED TO IGNORE THE MOLD ALTOGETHER...

at the vanguard, if at times unwittingly so. Certainly Slick more than once found herself far ahead of even the expectations a rock and roll crowd might have for a female lead singer. As she recalls, "Some guy at one concert in Chicago said—he thought he was being clever—and he said 'Hey Gracie, take off your chastity belt!' and I said, 'Chastity belt, hell, I don't even wear underpants!' and pulled up my skirt...and the band goes 'ugh.' But in the sixties we just took *all* the stuff off."

As more than one rock and roll chronicler has observed, Grace Slick was Ice and Janis Joplin was Fire. And, to paraphrase the 1968 hit by that name by the Crazy World of Arthur Brown, she'd teach you to burn. If female singers like Grace Slick broke the mold of the "chick" or girl singer, Janis Joplin

seemed to ignore the mold altogether...and, in so doing, become a hugely influential role model for several generations of women and women rock and roll musicians in particular. As Grace Slick puts it, "If the women were on the verge of just trying to move right up there to the fence and see what was going on then Janis was big enough, formidable enough to say, 'It can be done, it's OK, c'mon over'...so I think that she helped in that sense."

Janis's very appearance and demeanor were revolutionary for women at the time. She was not conventionally pretty—though many would call her deeply beautiful—and even in the early sixties in her home state of Texas, she seemed quietly determined not to accept the cookie-cutter niche that would be allowed her as a woman in the South.

As self-made sixties impresario Chet Helms remembers her before they both traveled to San Francisco together, "Janis was in a blue man's work shirt [and] pants at a time when women in Texas didn't wear pants...when every undergraduate at the University of Texas had a gray wool skirt, a white cotton blouse, white bobby sox, and penny loafers, and a bouffant hairdo. And Janis had her [hair] long and frizzy and wild and had a blue work shirt and blue jeans and little John Lennon glasses...and didn't wear a bra at a time when that was truly radical."

Or as Sam Andrew of Big Brother says of her later performing career, "Janis just by standing there on stage and singing those songs and doing that kind of thing and getting sweaty and dirty and ugly and putting it all out front, and that distortion in her voice...she was making a political statement."

Big Brother and the Holding Company—guitarists Sam Andrew and James Gurley, bass player Peter Albin, and drummer David Getz—had formed in 1965 under the influence and guidance of Chet Helms, whose Big Brother production company gave the band its name. In 1966, Helms brought Joplin into the band and the spark became a blues inferno.

Janis was born and raised in Port Arthur, Texas, a small city that was, in the 1950s, closer in spirit to Louisiana bayous across the Gulf than Lone Star plains. "Very removed in many ways from the monochromatic, well-modulated, suburban

THE EMERGENCE OF **COMPELLING NEW** FEMALE SINGERS **MADE IT A BANNER YEAR** FOR WOMEN WHO DID NOT **FIT THE TRADITIONAL MOLD** OF THE "CHICK SINGER." **DIVA PERHAPS; CHICK SINGER, NO.**

pink-and-gray land of Eisenhowerism, the blues sneaked into Janis's consciousness at the same time as her sexuality did—and that is no coincidence," remembers Sam Andrew, who, like Janis, hailed from this swampy part of East Texas.

It was a region where preachers railed against the "devil's music"—blues and rhythm and blues—while teenagers of all backgrounds discovered its erotic charge in the backseat of automobiles. It was that kind of place that was a crucible for the generational questioning of inherited beliefs that was helping to shake the country in 1968. As Andrew put it, "If the blues was forbidden and it turned out to be so good then what about sex in all of its many forms? What about cheap thrills, dope, living high?"

Those who heard her in those early years knew, as Andrew knew, that Janis wasn't just a white girl who sang the blues: She lived them, internalized them, and spewed them out in her own original, authentic way.

"You know, it's a good thing people like me the way I am, because I damn sure wouldn't know how to change," Janis said early in 1968. "I stomp on the tune like an elephant. I'm going for it...I'm going to shove the power right into you, right through you, and you can't refuse it. I'm going to give it all I got, and you know what? Why don't you do the same? Scream, yell, howl at the moon, man, tear it up, kick the door in, pound the walls, I'll be there doing it with you." Janis Joplin was clearly an artist in tune with her times.

Big Brother had exploded onto the San Francisco scene in the spring of 1967, when they stole the hearts of the crowd at the Monterey Pop Festival in northern California—the same event that made Jimi Hendrix a national figure and Otis Redding the soul hero for what he called "the love crowd."

In 1968, Big Brother released its second album, titled *Cheap Thrills,* a studio work recorded so as to have the ambience of a live show. The album boasted a memorable cover by San Francisco comic artist R. Crumb that became an instant piece of the sixties' visual iconography. And one song on that album in particular, "Piece of My Heart," became a generational anthem that spoke especially to the pain felt by so many women. As Chet Helms remembers Joplin's special interpretive gift, "I don't think Janis suffered any more or less than anybody else but I think Janis had the unique ability to get in touch with her pain and to express it in a way that was universally communicable and that we all identified with.

"I think there were a lot of women," Helms continues, "who were lying [in wait] for a certain freedom to explore areas that had always been reserved for men, and Janis didn't ask, she just took. She went. She did. She acted. And I think that was very appealing to a lot of women and I think rightfully so."

In 1968, Janis Joplin and Big Brother took a little piece of America's heart, as *Cheap Thrills* climbed the charts to become the number one album in the country. But almost coinciding with the chart triumph of *Cheap Thrills* and "Piece of My Heart" becoming a breakout hit single, Big Brother became the victim of both burnout and ambition.

"We worked a lot, maybe too much," Janis said at the time. "For two years now we've been playing almost every night and catching a lot of planes, doing the same old material. It gets harder to feel when it isn't fresh anymore and there's no time to write new stuff. Who wants to get paid ten grand for acting like you're having a good time? It kind of goes against everything we set out to do in the first place. The difference between me and them is that I saw it first. I love those guys but if I have any real sense of myself as a musician I have to move on."

Two years later, on October 4, 1970, Janis's body would be found in a Hollywood hotel room, dead of a heroin overdose. The album she had just completed, *Pearl,* would be the one that finally showed her at full maturity as a solo artist.

CHAPTER NINE

DARKNESS FALLS

 n understandable air of depression suffused the fall of 1968. As students returned to tense campuses, it was difficult to concentrate on books. Not only did the future look bleak and unappetizing, the present seemed downright dangerous.

For many, drugs helped. This may have been an autumn in which a majority of students at a majority of American campuses smoked marijuana regularly. Many took LSD or other hallucinogens occasionally. And some, like their rock and roll heroes, were beginning to use the hard drugs that would ultimately destroy the counterculture.

In October the epicenter of world student turmoil shifted to Mexico. Anger at overcrowding and irrelevance in the universities, corruption and decrepitude in the government had students in Mexico City and throughout the country marching in the streets during the summer.

As it happened, Mexico City was the host of the 1968 Summer Olympic Games that October. The government, autocratic and repressive in ordinary times, was determined that the games would proceed without any unsightly demonstrations.

On a hazy October night ten days before the games began, 8,000 students gathered for a pro-democracy rally in the capital's Tlatelolco Square. Dozens, and perhaps hundreds of them, did not live to tell about it. Government police and soldiers opened fire on the students, shooting indiscriminately on the ground and from sniper positions in and atop nearby buildings.

The government claimed—and still claims—that a Communist-leaning terror group called the Olympic Battalion had started the carnage. To this day, Mexicans of different political stripes blame their opposites. But most independent observers say it was government-sanctioned mass murder.

Ten days later on October 12, the Olympic Games started in Mexico City. And the year's passions made their way inside.

Two black Americans, Tommie Smith and John Carlos, won the gold and bronze medals in the 200-meter run. As they stood on the three-tiered

winners' boxes, as "The Star-Spangled Banner" played, Smith and Carlos bowed their heads and defiantly raised their fists over their heads in the Black Power salute. The integrity of the games had been violated, it was said. Smith and Carlos were made pariahs. Their medals were withdrawn, and they were kicked off the team.

But Black Power was fast becoming the dominant strain of the Civil Rights movement, especially now that the integration-minded leader Martin Luther King was gone. Prominent black Americans such as Muhammad Ali were even calling for black separatism, in another "state or territory."

Helping to fuel black pride, if not the separatist urges, was the release that fall of James Brown's "Say It Loud, I'm Black and I'm Proud." As disc jockey

Frank "Captain Al" Shefton remembers, "When James came out with 'Say It Loud, I'm Black and I'm Proud,' people sort of began to accept their blackness a little more, saying 'Well, James says this, and that's fine with me.'" Or as journalist Tim White puts it, "It was real as steel...that's why it was an anthem."

Though it is a generalization, it is not at all a reach to say that as the days grew shorter in 1968, the mood also grew darker. Vietnam remained a cancer on the body politic, with 540,000 U.S. troops there by the fall months. For the growing number of Americans who opposed the war, there seemed little hope that the year's presidential politics would bring a solution. Richard Nixon's promises of "peace with honor" seemed hollow at best, a

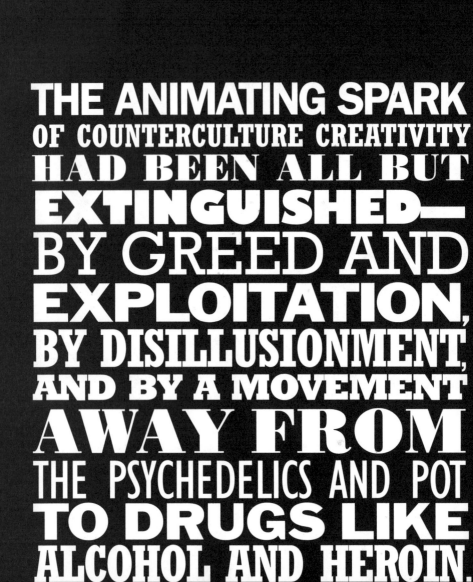

THE ANIMATING SPARK OF COUNTERCULTURE CREATIVITY HAD BEEN ALL BUT EXTINGUISHED— BY GREED AND EXPLOITATION, BY DISILLUSIONMENT, AND BY A MOVEMENT AWAY FROM THE PSYCHEDELICS AND POT TO DRUGS LIKE ALCOHOL AND HEROIN.

rationalization for escalating the war at worst. And with Democratic candidate Hubert Humphrey beholden to the Johnson administration's war policy, peace seemed a distant hope no matter what the eventual outcome of the November election.

The year's losses had begun to really sink in and the aftertaste was a bitter one. "Martin Luther King was shot, Bobby Kennedy was shot," remembers Grace Slick. "It's a hard time to have faith in the dream...because they keep picking off the leaders." And as Tim White points out, "The music just got darker," too, "it got darker across the board."

The change was exemplified by the apocalyptic sound of songs like "Time Has Come Today" by the Chambers Brothers. As Tim White recalls, "It sounded like it was your last chance to make a decision in terms of where you stood: 'Time has come today, young hearts must go their way, can't put it off another day'—y'know, you had to decide."

The huge popularity of the Doors in 1968, rock's dark poet princes, served to underscore this change.

Joan Didion's classic collection of essays about the dark undertow of the sixties, *The White Album,* captures the essential allure of the Doors in their place (southern California) and time, "an early spring evening" in 1968:

"The Doors were different...unconvinced that love was brotherhood. The Doors' music insisted that love was sex and sex was death and therein lay salvation."

Didion describes a scene in a recording studio during a session for the band's third album, *Waiting for the Sun*, in which band members Ray Manzarek, John Densmore, and Robbie Krieger, along with a bass player borrowed from the band Clear Light, are just sitting around.

But what they're waiting for is Jim Morrison, described by Didion as "a twenty-four-year-old graduate of UCLA who wore black vinyl pants and no underwear and tended to suggest some range of the possible just beyond a suicide pact."

Didion had picked up on culture clues that had not yet been clearly spelled out: That 1968 was a diabolically different year from the one that preceded it, that the "erotic politics" of the Doors were an endless winter away from 1967's Summer of Love.

Morrison had been arrested for public obscenity at a concert in New Haven in December 1967; in the cursed August of 1968, he was arrested for disorderly conduct on an airplane flight. And in 1968, Morrison was "the Lizard King," his "mythic alter ego." The band confronted the war in "The Unknown Soldier," and confronted the authorities in the menacing street-fighting anthem, "Five to One." Underlying the music and words of these songs was an eerie atmosphere that seemed to have in it much more of the devil than devil-may-care.

Former hippie enclaves, like San Francisco's Haight-Ashbury and New York's East Village, were also changing and not for the better. The animating spark of counterculture creativity that had made these places magnets for young people across the country had been all but extinguished—by greed and exploitation, by disillusionment, and by a movement away from the psychedelics and pot to drugs like alcohol and heroin.

As Dave Getz of Big Brother and the Holding Company recalls, "By the end of 1968, there were plenty of people drinking, there were plenty of hippies drinking, plenty of rock musicians drinking and starting to use cocaine and starting to use heroin a lot more."

Sam Andrew, also of Big Brother, adds, "You felt like, just in the whole society at large there was a turn for the worse there for a while. This initial inspirational phase was over with and then every-thing took a dive."

As the Election Day neared, the polls were showing Nixon and Humphrey in a dead heat. Nixon had used television to sock it to the liberals, students, and antiwar demonstrators that his tele-vision campaign ads portrayed as enemies of law

"NIXON GETTING ELECTED IN 1968 WAS JUST EXACTLY WHAT YOU WOULD EXPECT FROM AN EVIL BEAST LIKE AMERICA. IT JUST CONFIRMED OUR OPINION THAT THE COUNTRY WAS INSANE AND TERRIBLE AND SO ON AND SO FORTH."

and order. In his book *The Selling of the President 1968*, Joe McGinnis tells how the damaged goods that was Richard Nixon's political career was successfully repackaged through the power of television advertising.

The Nixon campaign staff hired a war-documentary filmmaker named Eugene Jones to make a series of commercials featuring provocative still photos and the words, though not the face, of the candidate.

Nixon read the words, lifted directly from his own convention acceptance speech, on the sound-track: "In recent years crime in this country has grown nine times as fast as the population. ...We owe it to the decent and law-abiding citizens of this country to take the offensive against the criminal forces that threaten their peace and security and to rebuild respect for law across this country. ..."

"There was nothing new in these words," McGinnis wrote. "But when the words were coupled with quickly flashing colored pictures of criminals, of policeman patrolling deserted streets, of bars on storefront windows, of disorder on a college campus, of peace demonstrators being led bleeding into a police van, then the words became something greater than what they actually were. It was the whole being greater than the sum of its parts."

This was television's version of "the New Nixon," the one to vote for if you wanted to put the hippies, the draft dodgers, black nationalists and their allies, the elitist college students, in their place.

When November 5 finally arrived, it had become clear that the stench of Chicago's tear gas had lingered too long over Humphrey's campaign. Richard Milhous Nixon won the presidency in one of the closest elections in American history.

For many young people in the antiwar movement, Nixon's election was the final, cruel blow of a relentless year. As John Fogerty says, "When Richard Nixon got elected, I was very disappointed... I really didn't even think [he] had a chance."

David Crosby looks back with more anger and frustration: "When they elected Richard Nixon, I could not help but be pissed off. We knew the guy was a crook. We knew he was a liar, we knew he was a complete sleazeball, and they elected him. ...That was the whole 'My America, right or wrong' gang saying, 'Dick Nixon, he'll fix it for us.' Dick Nixon couldn't fix a Kleenex box. You know? And what they were saying was 'We're not backing out of this war...we're going to kick those little Asiatic bastards in the butt.'"

P. J. O'Rourke notes that, for the left, "Nixon getting elected in 1968 was just exactly what you would expect from an evil beast like America. It just confirmed our opinion that the country was insane and terrible and so on and so forth." But "if somebody like Robert Kennedy or Gene McCarthy had been elected and then had to make all the compromises that Nixon had to make, of course, then we might have learned something. We might have realized just how complicated power in the Democracy is...it kept us from learning anything about politics."

Paul Kantner echoes this sentiment: "As Dan Quayle was the perfect foil for comedians, Nixon was the perfect foil for political activists...I mean, they couldn't have written better press releases to fight against Nixon's actions." For those who were speaking out against the war and the established order in song, Nixon's election even had an unexpected salutary effect: "It probably helped our record sales, if you want to get crass about it."

Kantner's Jefferson Airplane did, indeed, direct at least one important song against the "Nixonians," as Kantner terms them, in 1968—their searing hit "Crown of Creation" off the album of the same name. As he sees the song, "'Crown of

Creation' was sort of the beginning following ideas that led to the more openly...political tone of 'Volunteers' [the "Up Against the Wall, Motherfucker" song they would release in 1969]. It was the first sort of awareness that there are people aligned against you. In loyalty to their kind, they cannot tolerate our minds. And in loyalty to our kind, we cannot tolerate their opposition...a little more antagonistic than we had been before."

Musically, 1968 ended on a strong note. And there was a big surprise in store, as America's other "King," Elvis Presley, returned. The occasion? The December 3 Elvis Presley TV special.

Elvis, of course, had spent the 1960s sleepwalking through dozens of bland, forgettable movies and recording little other than the bland, forgettable songs on their soundtrack albums. But Presley had been the spark and focus of America's pop explosion. Greil Marcus and Charles Kaiser both note that the 1956 release of "Heartbreak Hotel" essentially created youth culture.

Presley was no rebel: He placidly accepted his drafting into the Army in 1958. In 1960, John F. Kennedy, forty-two, became president of the United States. Rich, articulate, photogenic, a man's man and a relentless seducer of women, JFK's election was a seeming triumph of youth culture.

When Kennedy was killed in 1963, no one knew what would become of the "new generation" to which a torch had been passed. The answer, as it turned out, would come from across the Atlantic.

Youth culture got a lift after the Kennedy assassination with the arrival of the Beatles' music at the end of 1963 and their physical arrival in the winter of 1964. Their music had a spontaneity and edge that had been missing from rock and pop since Presley's heyday. Their wit, charm, cute Liverpool accents, and eccentric mop-top haircuts made them immediately beloved, ushered in the English Invasion in rock and roll, and seemed to set off a creative fury in pop music that reached what may be a never-to-be-matched peak in 1968.

The Beatles and Rolling Stones had a friendly rivalry for supremacy that was also at a pinnacle in the autumn of 1968 with the overlapping releases of the albums *The Beatles* (aka *The White Album*) and *Beggars Banquet*. In fact, these albums would show the groups moving in two directions: the Beatles toward what was by then their inevitable breakup, while the Stones consolidated their position as "the world's greatest rock band." (A title granted under the assumption that the Beatles' greatness transcended "rock.")

The Beatles remained largely remote from each other after returning from their disillusioning retreat with their guru, the Maharishi, in India early in 1968. *The White Album,* as it came to be known because of its plain white cover, was a two-album set.

During the summer, the Beatles appeared in a full-length movie—as cartoon characters. The animated film *Yellow Submarine* featured Beatles music in a visually enchanting setting. The film's story told of how the Fab Four saved fictional "Pepperland" from bad guys called Blue Meanies, which looked to many in the counterculture like cops.

In September, the Beatles released what may have been their most lasting single, the lengthy tour de force "Hey Jude." This gorgeous spiritual ballad, sung by Paul McCartney, carried a message of healing, but a subtext that suggested an inevitable parting. On the flip side was "Revolution," inspired by the Paris riots, on which John Lennon cautioned raging politicos: "If you go around carrying pictures of Chairman Mao/You ain't gonna make it with anyone anyhow."

The White Album, released in December, had the texture of songs by four solo artists rather than one focused, interacting group. Nevertheless, it was a triumph.

Perhaps *The White Album* was primarily escapism, the Beatles forging entertainment with a personal touch rather than writing manifestos to the rebels in the streets. But the Rolling Stones had their ears very carefully tuned to the streets, and on *Beggars Banquet,* they roused the rebel culture of 1968 with a marching, charging masterpiece.

Though neither "Sympathy for the Devil" nor "Street Fighting Man" were released as singles, they are among the most prominent Stones tracks. "Sympathy" had become, in rewrite, the Stones' iconoclastic reaction to the year of assassinations. "I shouted out, 'Who killed the Kennedys?'/When

after all, it was you and me," Mick Jagger sang. On "Street Fighting Man," the Stones seized the political moment, capturing the visceral impulse to riot while maintaining their own distance from violent action. "But what can a poor boy do/but to sing in a rock and roll band?" the song asked.

Elsewhere on the album, however, the Stones showed how versatile a rock and roll band could be. Keith Richards's "No Expectations" had such Appalachian dirt under its fingernails that it was covered by a number of hard-ass country singers. "Prodigal Son" nearly materializes the ghost of Robert Johnson, while "Stray Cat Blues" was leering cock-rock for the ages.

With the Beatles and Stones at full force, it seemed a miracle that the man who made them possible showed up at all.

Elvis Presley wasn't dead during the 1960s, but he might as well have been. (Seething with resentment at having been displaced, he even snubbed the Beatles when they came to visit the King's Hollywood Hills home.)

Reviewing *This Is Elvis,* a revealing semi-documentary released in 1981, critic Roger Ebert grasped the spiritual pallor Presley projected in the 1960s. "The charisma stays," Ebert notes. "But somewhere along the way we notice a change in his behavior, a draining away of cheerfulness, a dreadful secret scourge."

In 1965, Bob Dylan had released *Highway 61 Revisited,* one of the greatest rock albums of all time; the Beatles released the soundtrack to their hit movie, *Help!*; and the Rolling Stones put out two of their best albums, *Out of Our Heads* and *December's Children.*

Three Elvis Presley albums were released in 1965 as well: the compilation *Elvis for Everyone!* and the soundtracks *Girl Happy* and *Harum Scarum.* It seemed as if the King's moment had irrevocably passed.

By 1968, the descent seemed bottomless. And Elvis had never seemed so out of touch with the tenor of the times. Ten days after the Tet Offensive,

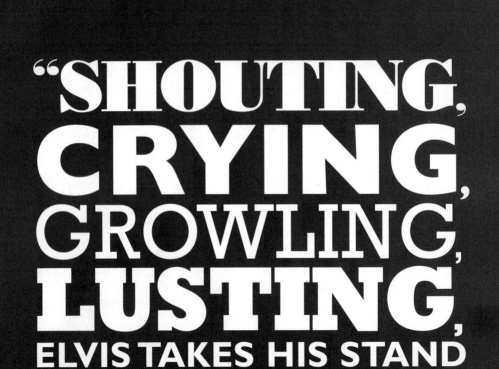

"**SHOUTING, CRYING, GROWLING, LUSTING,** ELVIS TAKES HIS STAND

the Elvis movie soundtrack *Clambake* peaked at #40 on the *Billboard* chart.

Was Elvis finished? The December 3, 1968 concert might have been his last chance to avoid total irrelevance and rescue his legacy. Elvis's manager, the notorious Colonel Tom Parker, wanted Presley in a tuxedo singing Christmas songs. This time, the usually docile Presley, backed by producer Steve Binder, got up the gumption to say no. He wanted to rock again. In what may be the best essay ever written about the King—"Elvis: Presliad," in the book *Mystery Train*—author Greil Marcus sets the scene and assesses the stakes:

"Sitting on a stage in black leather, surrounded by friends and a rough little combo, the crowd buzzing, he sang and talked and joked, and all the resentments he had hidden over the years began to pour out. He had always said yes, but this time he was saying no—not without humor, but almost

with a wry bit of guilt, as if he had betrayed his talent and himself. 'Been a long time, baby.'"

Marcus keys in on the version of "One Night" Presley sang that evening. Elvis's 1958 hit was a cleaned-up version of Smiley Lewis's bawdy R&B song, known originally as "One Night (of Sin)." With everything on the line, Presley sang Smiley Lewis's version, as if he knew that what was once good enough would no longer pass:

"Shouting, crying, growling, lusting, Elvis takes his stand and the crowd takes theirs with him, no longer reaching for the past they had been brought to the studio to reenact, but responding to something completely new. It was the finest music of his life. If ever there was music that bleeds, this was it."

If it turned out to be an all-too fleeting triumph for Elvis, it was a fitting coda for the year that bled.

CHAPTER TEN

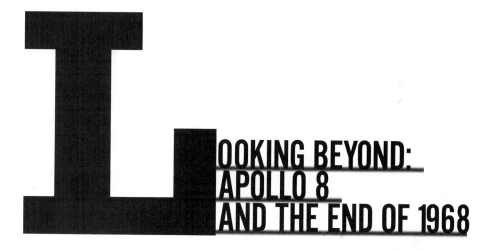

LOOKING BEYOND: APOLLO 8 AND THE END OF 1968

uring the last ten days of 1968, three men had the chance to leave the atmosphere that had grown so heavy to so many. The name of this power trio was Frank Borman, James Lovell, and William Anders, American astronauts. Early on the morning of December 21, 1968, as millions of Americans were beginning their Christmas holiday travels, this crew for the mission designated Apollo 8 blasted off from Florida's Kennedy Space Center en route to orbit the moon.

THINGS ON EARTH HAD BEEN SO TOUCHY DURING 1968 THAT SOME IN THE SPACE PROGRAM RECOMMENDED POSTPONING THE MISSION.

In any other year, this might have been cause for celebration. But the ongoing Vietnam War and the accompanying disdain for anything to do with the government or military made this at first an anticlimactic mission.

But the mission provided a transcendent moment of reflection as the Apollo 8 crew viewed the ball of Earth from space. Mission Control heard astronaut Jim Lovell sharing a thought with Borman:

"Frank, what I keep imagining is if I am some lonely traveler from another planet what I would think about the earth at this altitude, whether I think it would be inhabited or not...I was just curious if I would land on the blue or brown part of the Earth."

Things on Earth had been so touchy during 1968 that some in the space program recommended postponing the mission. A space disaster around Christmas would have been devastating to the public in any year. In 1968, such a tragedy might have been a blow that the nation's psyche might not have been able to withstand.

But as Apollo 8 circled the moon on Christmas Eve, a bit of much-needed gladness filled many hearts. On one orbit, Frank Borman recited a prayer, which went, in part:

Give us, O God, the vision which can see thy love in the world in spite of human failure.

Give us the faith to trust thy goodness in spite of our ignorance and weakness.

Give us the knowledge that we may continue to pray with understanding hearts.

And show us what each one of us can do to set forward the coming of the day of universal peace. Amen.

A few orbits later, the Apollo 8 crew read from the Book of Genesis, in a moment seen and heard all over the world, closing with the blessing: "Good night, good luck, a Merry Christmas, and God bless all of you—all of you on the good Earth."

A few hours later, on Christmas morning, Apollo 8 was still orbiting the moon. Reverting to military jargon, Jim Lovell sent this dispatch to Mission Control.

"Please be informed that there is a Santa Claus."

The traumas of 1968 lingered for years to come. Abbie Hoffman, Jerry Rubin, and five others were indicted by the government on conspiracy charges for their role in the Chicago convention riots. The 1970 trial, with the cranky and utterly biased Judge Julius Hoffman presiding, was a low point in American jurisprudence.

The Vietnam War would continue seven more years. "When we started to protest," says David Crosby, "we thought we'd have it over in a year." Some protestors, like the radical Weather Underground, would turn to terrorism, detonating bombs, robbing banks, and killing the innocent along with themselves. President Nixon, flexing his law and order muscles, was unapologetic when American soldiers, members of the Ohio National Guard, opened fire on students protesting his bombing of Cambodia in May 1970 at prototypically middle-American Kent State University, killing four of them.

The fall of Saigon in 1975 signified the first major military defeat suffered by the United States in its then 199-year history.

Many of Martin Luther King's dreams of peace and progress have gone unfulfilled. Though many blacks have achieved prosperity, cities like Detroit and Newark still bear the deep scars of the riots that leveled them.

"I THINK THE WORLD WAS **CHANGED** IN A VERY SMALL WAY **BY MUSIC.** AND I THINK THAT WE HAVE **HELPED PEOPLE** BE LESS ALONE. WE HAVE HELPED THEM **TO BE LESS CRAZY.**"

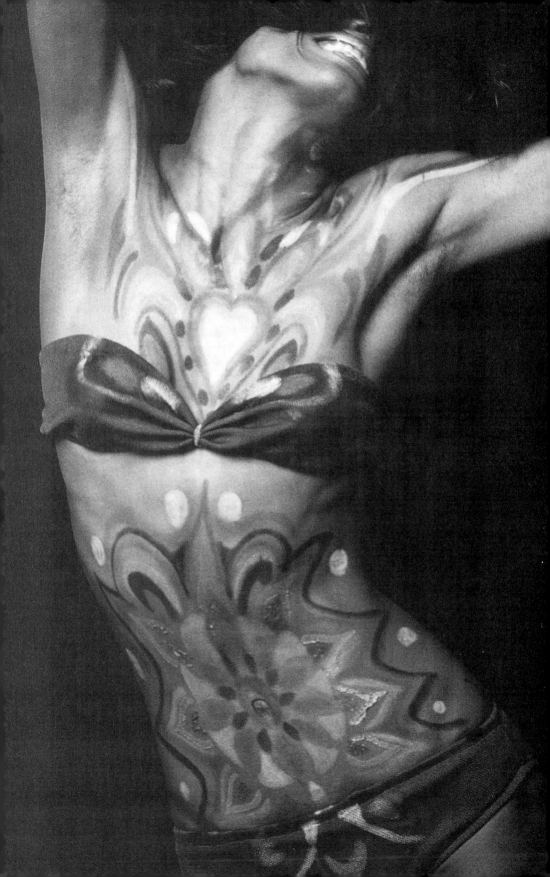

Yet there were some positives that came out of 1968. Many of them were musical.

They could, in fact, build an entire wing onto the Rock and Roll Hall of Fame just to honor the music of 1968. There may never be another year in which you'll hear pop music with the breadth, depth, excitement, and innovation it achieved in 1968. As Tim White succinctly understates it, "...1968 was...a good vintage in music."

The Beatles peaked, the Rolling Stones reigned, the Doors, the Jefferson Airplane, and the Grateful Dead gelled. The Mothers of Invention and the Fugs were flat-out outrageous.

The Jimi Hendrix Experience and Cream proved that a trio could make a mighty noise, taking the blues out of the country and into the adrenaline city.

Janis Joplin, with Big Brother and the Holding Company, and Grace Slick, with the Jefferson Airplane, showed that a confident, bold woman could lead a nasty rock and roll band.

Creedence Clearwater Revival brought rock back to its basics while finding a metaphor for these war years in the Louisiana swamp. Dr. John, a veteran musical hipster out of New Orleans, gave those swamps a psychedelic bath.

There was also a backlash, reflected in the year's charts. A focal point of the "counter-counter-culture" may have been Glen Campbell. A prominent L.A. studio musician (with the Beach Boys and on many Phil Spector hits), the clean-cut Campbell became a symbol of the silent majority with his hit TV show, which began in 1968 and ran through 1972.

Following the success of "By the Time I Get to Phoenix" in 1967, Campbell's middle-of-the-road country-flavored songs in 1968, like "Dreams of the Everyday Housewife," gave him great appeal to those who opposed the war. And his 1968 hit, Jimmy Webb's gorgeously written "Wichita Lineman," celebrated the small-town values that were overlooked and sometimes mocked by the hippie revolution. Campbell tapped into some strong feelings: He had six albums on the charts in 1968.

Also big, leaning on the right side of the middle of the road, were mawkish country-pop ballads like "Honey" by Bobby Goldsboro, a number one single for five weeks in the late winter and spring. Jeannie C. Riley's "Harper Valley P.T.A." also crossed over from the country side, but it was a novelty song with a subversive streak: It poked fun at the hypocrisy rife in small-town America.

For soul music it was a watershed year. James Brown was all over the place. Otis Redding's posthumous "(Sittin' On) The Dock of the Bay" was a huge hit. "Love Child," by Diana Ross and the Supremes, was an example of topical songwriting penetrating even Motown. For escapism, you had to go to Philadelphia, from which Archie Bell and the Drells sent out the call to "Tighten Up." Marvin Gaye's "I Heard It Through the Grapevine," meanwhile, shows how even songs of unrequited love had an ominous feel in 1968.

"I think the world was changed in a very small way by music," asserts Graham Nash. "And I think that we have helped people be less alone. We have helped them to be less crazy."

Country Joe McDonald agrees. "We did make a dream come true for ourselves. And the dream was not about money, and it was not about style. It was about your heart and the way you live and society and the way we all live together."

But others are not so sure, and regret their own naivete and the absurdity of what they thought they could accomplish. "I was dumb enough to think, if you take psychedelics and if you read enough books, that intellectually you can change the dynamism of human aggression," says Grace Slick, now in her fifties and sober.

Big Brother's Dave Getz sees it differently: "Nineteen sixty-eight was a good year, where I had that sense of really being in history...having that sense that...this is a transcendent moment...and an important moment in history."

P. J. O'Rourke, however, mocks the preten-

"THE IDEALISM OF 1968 WASN'T **OFF BASE.** PEOPLE HAD REAL FEARS... THE MERE FACT THAT **THIRTY YEARS LATER** WE'RE TALKING ABOUT A LOT OF THIS MUSIC **[PROVES THAT]** **IT REALLY WAS** **AND REMAINS** THE CONSCIENCE OF A **CULTURE**."

sions of those who thought music could save the world. "It thought it was a method of achieving spiritual truth, and political justice around the world. This is vaudeville. Why would guitar players save the world?"

Tim White, though, sees 1968 as "the beginning of the time when things like the pop music charts...would start to seem like a yardstick for how people were feeling."

"You know," he holds today, "the idealism of 1968 wasn't off base. People had real fears and these fears have been mounting steadily since Dwight Eisenhower gave that speech warning about the military industrial complex...I think the mere fact that thirty years later we're talking about a lot of this music [proves that] it really was and remains the conscience of a culture." Looking at the legacy of 1968, and its music, White says, "This

music has endured, and we're all still here, at least a lot of us are. And the business is still unfinished. And that's our problem."

Paul Kantner may have the best take on the turbulent year that was 1968: "George Bernard Shaw said something to the effect that, 'The reasonable man adapts himself to his environment. The unreasonable man tries to adapt his environment to himself. Therefore, all progress in civilization is made by the unreasonable man.' And we were very definitely, in 1967, the unreasonable people. And in 1968, we got a little bit of reason that we should take care of what's coming over the hillside, but [we also held] on to [those] unreasonable expectations."

It was 1968—the year reason met with unreason, and produced some of the most enduring music of our time.

Acknowledgments

Thanks to Paul Gallagher for putting in the time and pulling this whole series together.

Special thanks to the following: Liz Brooks, Dave Dunton, Wallie Einenkel, Jeff Gaspin, Monica Halpert, Jacob Hoye, Jonathan Hyams at Michael Ochs Archives, Dean Lubensky, Lisa Masuda, Jill Modabber, JoAnna Myers, George Moll, Natasha O'Connor at Magnum Photos, Donna O'Neill, Red Herring Design, Gay Rosenthal, Ann Sarnoff, Paul Schnee, Lisa Silfen, Robin Silverman, Donald Silvey, Liate Stehlik, John Sykes, Wendy Walker, Kara Welsh, Eric Wybenga and, finally, Bill Flanagan and Gerald Leo, who wrote the original overview for the show.

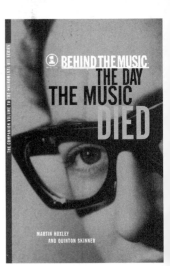